A LEGACY OF DISCRIMINATION

The Essential Constitutionality of Affirmative Action

Lee C. Bollinger

AND

Geoffrey R. Stone

OXFORD
UNIVERSITY PRESS

Oxford University Press is a department of the University of Oxford. It furthers
the University's objective of excellence in research, scholarship, and education
by publishing worldwide. Oxford is a registered trade mark of Oxford University
Press in the UK and certain other countries.

Published in the United States of America by Oxford University Press
198 Madison Avenue, New York, NY 10016, United States of America.

© Oxford University Press 2023

CIP data is on file at the Library of Congress

ISBN 978–0–19–768574–7

DOI: 10.1093/oso/9780197685747.001.0001

1 3 5 7 9 8 6 4 2
Printed by Sheridan Books, Inc., United States of America

To Jean and Jane
And to the next generation:
Cooper, Sawyer, Katelyn, Colin, and Emma
Julie, Mollie, Maddie, Jackson, Bee, and Leni

The title of our volume is inspired by Justice Thurgood Marshall's incisive dissent in *Regents of the University of California v. Allan Bakke* (1978), in which he stated:

I agree with the judgment of the Court only insofar as it permits a university to consider the race of an applicant in making admissions decisions. I do not agree that petitioner's admissions program violates the Constitution. For it must be remembered that, during most of the past 200 years, the Constitution as interpreted by this Court did not prohibit the most ingenious and pervasive forms of discrimination against the Negro. Now, when a State acts to remedy the effects of that legacy of discrimination, I cannot believe that this same Constitution stands as a barrier.

CONTENTS

ACKNOWLEDGMENTS

We acknowledge and express our deepest gratitude to the following people: Jack Dougherty provided multiple drafts and research for the story to be told, with support from Matthew Beckwith, Claire Levenson, and Andrew Sanger. Walter Dellinger—our longtime friend and colleague, who died tragically in February 2022—and his colleague Jonathan Hacker, with the assistance of Grace Leeper, at the distinguished law firm O'Melveny, helped us build and fill out the legal background for the thesis of the book. Jane Booth, general counsel of Columbia University, and Shailagh Murray, executive vice president for public affairs of Columbia University, provided their own wonderful counsel and a link with these colleagues. The Office of the President at Columbia and especially Christina Shelby, senior executive director, gave indispensable organization to the project.

Many people, far too many to acknowledge here, have contributed greatly to the ideas set forth in this volume. Two colleagues merit special notice: Claude Steele (Lucie Stern Professor Emeritus of Psychology at Stanford University) and Ira Katznelson (Ruggles

Professor of Political Science and History at Columbia University), for their support, comments, and, in each case, profoundly important scholarship on which we rely in the pages that follow. The brilliant Reconstruction era scholarship of Eric Foner (DeWitt Clinton Professor Emeritus of History at Columbia University) is also foundational to this work. And, as always, our spouses: Jean Magnano Bollinger, who offered inspiration, fortification, and substance;[1] and Jane Dailey, professor of American history and the College at the University of Chicago, who shared her insightful historical knowledge.[2]

The intent of this book is to give readers a primer on affirmative action and its larger context and to develop a constitutional theory for it. As such, it represents our views and ours alone.

Introduction

"Affirmative action."

These two words, considered separately, sound positive, even benign. Yet as a phrase, they spark visceral reactions across American society. Some believe we do not have enough of it; others believe we have too much of it. Nearly everyone who has applied for a job or admission to a selective college or university has an opinion about affirmative action, ranging from enthusiastic support to fierce opposition.

The term gained currency in the early 1960s, during the civil rights era. President John F. Kennedy introduced the concept in Executive Order No. 10925, signed on March 6, 1961.[1] The order included a provision that government contractors "take affirmative action to ensure that applicants are employed, and employees are treated [fairly] during employment, without regard to their race, creed, color, or national origin."[2]

What fair-minded person could object to that?

But what began as a good-faith effort to expand opportunities to Americans who had historically been denied them—especially Black Americans—soon became defined, in the minds of some, as preferential treatment for some groups at the expense of others.

How did an effort to level the playing field for *all* Americans come to be interpreted by some Americans as a zero-sum game— a ruthless competition for coveted positions in schools and workplaces, with clear winners and losers? Further, given that six decades after President Kennedy signed his executive order and that many segments of the population still encounter discrimination as a result of their race, creed, color, and national origin, where do we go from here?

In this short book we passionately, and, we hope, convincingly, argue that Black Americans—despite emancipation from slavery, despite Supreme Court decisions such as *Brown v. Board of Education,* and despite congressional legislation upholding the right to vote and other progress made since the civil rights era—still do not compete with their fellow countrymen and women on a level playing field. We argue that this nation's obligation to remediate past discrimination based on race is far from over. And we contend that conscience and jurisprudence not only can but must be intertwined to advance and protect the American ideals we claim to cherish. Affirmative action, we hold, is not only constitutionally permissible, it is morally mandated. It is the *right* thing to do as well as the *just* thing to do.

Critics of affirmative action—even those who would concede that everything we have asserted about the lack of a level educational and economic playing field in the United States may, in fact, be true—decouple conscience and jurisprudence. They argue that under the Equal Protection Clause of the Fourteenth Amendment, which prohibits selective denial of rights on the basis of race,[3] our nation should not constitutionally permit the state to take race into account even for the noblest of reasons because the state, when granted that authority in the past, abused it for centuries. Given the effort it took to unwind three centuries' worth of race-based law, why, they ask, would we *ever* want to re-empower the state in that realm—even if for ostensibly good reasons? Accordingly, they assert, any exception to or workaround within the Fourteenth Amendment is unacceptable and should be strictly prohibited.

We disagree. It is possible both to comply with the language and essential purpose of the Fourteenth Amendment and to allow the state to create truly equal opportunity for all Americans. Indeed, the "risk" that the government would abuse its capacity to do good is in our view an overstated risk, a classic slippery slope argument which assumes that if we crack the door open a bit further for good reasons that invariably means the government will begin applying race-conscious policies for bad reasons. But this logic relies on an assumption that American jurists—not to mention legislators, educators, news media commentators, civil rights activists, and 331 million citizens—will not be able to tell the difference between good reasons and bad ones. Further, why is the burden placed on affirmative action proponents to expressly show there will not be such harm, as opposed to challenging affirmative action opponents to show that there will be?

Is it not better to confront injustice and expect to modify and course correct in real time as required, rather than protect and defend an unjust status quo?

Given the composition of the Supreme Court at the time of this writing, there is temptation among affirmative action's supporters to engage in hand-wringing over the fate of the policy. We resist this temptation. Time and again, the American judicial system has demonstrated that it has the capacity to engage the ever-shifting American story, shrewdly recognizing when pivotal social and political inflection points have arrived and when past and present need to be reconciled to forge a more just society.

As debates over affirmative action are waged in the coming decade—in state legislatures, at the ballot box, in courtrooms and classrooms, in the media, and at the kitchen table—America will be presented with a once-in-a-generation opportunity to reassert its commitment to advancing opportunity, dignity, and equality for all Americans, for generations to come.

Will the Court and the country deliver on their promise to enable Black Americans to access education and related social mobility denied them for centuries? Will higher education be enabled or obstructed in those efforts?

We explore these questions, and many more, in this book. We examine affirmative action's original intent, impact, and future prospects. We discuss the role the courts played in shaping both American attitudes about, and outcomes related to, affirmative action. Our focus, generally, is on the law and, in particular, its impact on Black Americans and other historically disadvantaged groups. In addition to evaluating the content of judicial decisions, we also explore the ever-changing social and historical contexts in which race-related rulings were, currently are, and are in the future likely to be forged.

We begin our story in post-emancipation America, with the passage of the three Reconstruction amendments to the federal Constitution: the Thirteenth, the Fourteenth, and the Fifteenth. The Civil War settled the question whether a state could secede from the Union, and the Thirteenth Amendment (1865) ended slavery. The Fifteenth Amendment (1870) guaranteed the right of adult men to vote without discrimination on the basis of race, color, or previous condition of servitude. But the question whether individual citizens had any federal constitutional rights against the states remained unresolved. Before the Civil War, the Constitution guaranteed individual rights only against the federal government. After the Union

victory, however, the Fourteenth Amendment (1868) expressly defined national citizenship and prohibited any state from depriving
any person of "life, liberty or property without due process of law,"
from denying any citizen the "privileges and immunities" of citizenship, and from denying any person "the equal protection of the
laws." Section 5 of the amendment authorized Congress to enforce
these guarantees through "appropriate legislation."[4]

In principle, the United States appeared to be committed to
remediating past injustices. In practice, though, repeated efforts
to advance equality for Black Americans were met, for the next
fifteen years, with resistance, as the Supreme Court, in one case
after another, narrowly interpreted the Fourteenth Amendment's
guarantees. For example, in the *Slaughter-House Cases* (1873),[5]
a landmark decision that held that the Privileges or Immunities
Clause of the Fourteenth Amendment only protects legal rights associated with federal U.S. citizenship—not those pertaining to state
citizenship—a bitterly divided Court, in a 5-4 decision, rendered
the "privileges or immunities" Clause essentially meaningless. In
that decision, the justices restricted the rights promised under the
Fourteenth Amendment, contending that they were not applicable
to all Americans but only to formerly enslaved persons.[6]

In 1875 Congress passed civil rights legislation prohibiting discrimination against Black Americans at inns, restaurants, theaters,
and other public venues; seven years later, the Supreme Court, in
the *Civil Rights Cases*,[7] ruled the legislation unconstitutional. The
Fourteenth Amendment, said the Court, disallowed racial discrimination as practiced by the states, but private individuals were
free to continue discriminating against Black Americans if it was
"local custom."[8] And custom it was, in a large swath of the country:
Discrimination against Black Americans continued, unregulated
and unconstrained. This hair-splitting by the Court was greeted with

indignation by proponents of racial equality, who pointed out that the lines between the public and the private spheres were blurred daily in American life, since transportation services, restaurants, and scores of other privately owned businesses were regulated by governmental authorities.[9]

Further, the Fifteenth Amendment may have guaranteed the right to vote to Black men, but the states were allowed latitude to define their electorates for themselves. Eleven former Confederate states seized this opportunity with gusto, and rewrote their constitutions to include new provisions calling for the establishment of byzantine voter-registration protocols, white primaries, literacy tests and poll taxes, and other measures intended to nullify not only the votes of Black men, but also the votes of white men who supported racial equality. Since white and Black prospective voters were both required to navigate the same obstacle course, the Supreme Court, in 1898, ruled in *Williams v. Mississippi* that poll taxes and literacy tests did not violate the Fifteenth Amendment.[10]

And in what was to become the most historically significant case of the era, in *Plessy v. Ferguson* (1896), which we discuss in greater detail in Chapter 2, the Court, in an 8-1 decision, upheld the notion that state-dictated "equal but separate" railway cars for Black and white passengers were consistent with the Fourteenth Amendment. The Court explained, "We consider the underlying fallacy of the plaintiff's argument to consist in the assumption that the enforced separation of the two races stamps the colored race with a badge of inferiority. If this is so, it is not by reason of anything found in the act, but solely because the colored race chooses to put that construction upon it."[11]

Emboldened by one Supreme Court victory after another, states and municipalities nationwide—especially, but not exclusively, in the South—enacted even more of what would become known as Jim Crow laws, all of them designed not only to keep the races separate but to push Black Americans to the margins of American society. In the decades that followed, state and local laws decreed that Black and white Americans could not be educated at the same schools, be treated in the same hospitals, drink from the same water fountains, or be buried in the same cemeteries.

For the purposes of a short book focused on affirmative action in higher education, our story turns next to the most significant Supreme Court decision of the last century, *Brown v. Board of Education of Topeka, Kansas* (1954), in which the Court overruled *Plessy* and its logic in the realm of public education.[12] We then follow desegregation and affirmative action's turbulent journey—and Black and white Americans' equally turbulent journey—through the decades that followed, up to the present day, when, in the aftermath of the 2020 police murder of George Floyd, nearly everyone in America, not only people of color, engaged in one of the most serious and urgent reckonings over race in the nation's history.

In Chapter 1 we analyze *Brown* in depth before pivoting to an examination of American society's varied responses to the decision, from expected outcomes such as southern resistance to integration, to unanticipated developments such as white flight from cities, which began in earnest in the 1950s and continued for decades. We discuss how, in the aftermath of *Brown*, a growing civil rights movement kept questions of racial inequality before Congress, the courts, and the American people. Civil rights lawyers like Thurgood Marshall and his colleagues with the Legal Defense Fund of the National Association for the Advancement of Colored Persons (NAACP) took on not only legally sanctioned de jure discrimination but also the many forms of de facto discrimination that continued to oppress Black Americans. This includes the sweeping reforms of the 1960s from the Civil Rights Act of 1964 to the Voting

Rights Act of 1965, *Loving v. Virginia* in 1967, which reversed state bans on interracial marriage, and the Fair Housing Act of 1968.[13]

Brown was a truly seminal Supreme Court decision that had profound effects throughout constitutional law, our laws and public policies, and our understandings of ourselves as American citizens. So, as scholars of the First Amendment, we turn next to tracing how freedom of speech and press were reformulated, indeed re-created, during the 1960s, on a parallel track in the context of the civil rights movement, as efforts to limit the speech of ministers, thwart protesters from assembling, prevent civil rights groups from litigating, and chill race-related press reporting were confronted at every turn. Many of the key First Amendment cases of the era were civil rights cases as much as they were pure freedom of speech or press cases, among them the landmark *New York Times Co. v. Sullivan* (1964), a showdown between a white supremacist Alabama city commissioner and the *New York Times*—and, indirectly, the Court itself.[14]

As we will describe, at nearly every step along the journey to advance opportunity for Black Americans, friction arose between those who believed the nation was not doing enough to redress past wrongs and those who believed the nation was over-correcting. As the 1960s gave way to the 1970s, however, more controversy erupted, this time over the issue of school busing, which culminated in the 1971 Supreme Court decision *Swann v. Charlotte-Mecklenburg Board of Education*.[15]

By the mid-1970s, it was increasingly evident to many Americans that the dreams of *Brown* were not by any means being fully realized. As primary and secondary school desegregation efforts were resisted, public and private colleges and universities across the country took stock of the continued lack of presence of Black students in their own classrooms and libraries. Affirmative action policies were thus formulated and adopted in order to increase minority representation in their institutions, which opened the next contentious chapter in the story: the ongoing debate, and litigation, over college and university admissions practices.

Chapter 2 presents a history of legal rulings and discusses the extent to which they either advanced or retarded efforts to promote racial equity in America. A key case to be examined in this chapter is *University of California v. Bakke* (1978),[16] which shaped the contours of private attitudes, public discourse, and the Court's affirmative action decision making for the next four decades. *Bakke* reflected a dramatic reframing of affirmative action's original intent: from improving opportunities for Black students to ensuring that *all* students (the majority of them white) would experience increased exposure to Black and other minority students and thus accrue "the general benefits of diversity."[17] This legal shift from questions of equity to education, spearheaded by Justice Lewis Powell's opinion in the *Bakke* decision, in effect sanitized the entire project. The shift also anticipated—or perhaps reflected—the backlash against affirmative action that continues to this day.

In Chapter 2 we also take readers on a journey through the Reagan era, the 1990s, and into the new millennium, during a time when affirmative action's proponents faced steep uphill climbs in both courts of law and the court of public opinion. During these years, colleges and universities were confronted with ever more litigation. Statewide ballot initiatives seeking either to limit affirmative action policies or dismantle them outright popped up nationwide and were passed by voters by wide majorities.

Against this backdrop, we describe how higher education resolved to become more strategic and aggressive in response to what it perceived as an existential threat to its mission. The centerpiece of the chapter is the *Grutter v. Bollinger* decision of 2003, which became *the* landmark decision on affirmative action in higher education—the first case in which a majority of the Court adopted a unified position holding affirmative action constitutional under the Fourteenth Amendment.[18] But the outcome of this case—and other Supreme Court cases that followed—were qualified victories for affirmative action's proponents. In *Grutter*, for example, Justice Sandra Day O'Connor, writing for the majority, authored a "sunset clause" on racism in America. By the year 2028, she contended, puzzlingly, America would be colorblind.[19]

In *Gratz v. Bollinger*, also decided in 2003, the Court left the door open for the University of Michigan and other universities to continue to use racial preferences to promote diversity as one of many determinants, but not the sole determinant, of admission.[20] *Fisher v. University of Texas* ("*Fisher I*"), decided in 2013, ruled that strict scrutiny—whereby the constitutional validity of a law or policy may be upheld only if the government can demonstrate in court that the law or regulation is necessary to achieve a "compelling state interest"—must be "narrowly tailored" to achieve the compelling purpose and that the "least restrictive means" to achieve the purpose should be applied to determine the constitutionality of a race-sensitive admissions policy.[21] A follow-up case, "*Fisher II*" (2016), which ruled that the University of Texas's use of race in its admissions policy passed constitutional muster, underscored the Court's desire to consider racial diversity only in terms of its educational benefit.[22] For the first two decades of the twenty-first century, the Court may have protected the affirmative action status quo, but in its rulings it steadfastly refused to acknowledge the persistent pertinence of race, and racial discrimination, in America, which defined the context in which its rulings were issued.

Chapter 3 examines the experience of Black Americans today, focusing on both the progress achieved since *Brown* and obstacles remaining. To be sure, we assert, the nation fared better with *Brown* and affirmative action than without it: Colleges, professional schools, and other academic disciplines became more racially diverse, in turn increasing diversity across the ranks of doctors, lawyers, journalists, business owners, and other professionals. The entrenched white male elite that had steered America's leading institutions for centuries was finally compelled to make room at the table for an emergent and diverse meritocracy that included white women, non-Christians, and people of color. To some observers, these signs of progress were touted as evidence that the journey for equality was, if not completed, advancing steadily and admirably.

But others, particularly those attentive to racial disparities in everything from high school graduation rates to mass incarceration and police violence, were determined to draw the nation's eyes to ongoing racial inequality and discrimination, especially after the formation of the Black Lives Matter movement in 2013 and the murder of George Floyd, an unarmed Black man at the hands of a white police officer in 2020. Supporters of ongoing efforts to lessen racial discrimination shined a light on recent state and federal measures that contravened the Voting Rights Act of 1965. Despite *Brown's* commitment to integrated schools, they wondered why, over the course of a quarter century, from 1988 to 2014, the number of K-12 schools in the United States that had a 99 percent nonwhite student population tripled.[23] They questioned why Black men and women— who comprised 13 percent of the U.S. population—comprised less than 8 percent of the white-collar workforce but more than a third of Americans incarcerated in prisons.[24] They reminded America that Black Americans, more than any other group, still endured discrimination, not only by the police but in employment, access to credit and capital, access to housing, access to quality educational and healthcare facilities, and, indeed, across virtually every facet of their lives.

In Chapter 4, we assert that affirmative action remains worthy of defense and protection, because, for millions of Black Americans, the dream of equal social, economic, and educational opportunity remains a dream deferred. It is important to note that the roots of affirmative action as a form of redress for racial injustice took hold during the Reconstruction era, under the direction of Black and white Republicans. Moreover, in the 1920s through the 1940s, this understanding of justice expanded, in what would be called "the Black Freedom Movement," to include interracially coordinated efforts to champion equality for Black Americans, and bloomed with the *Brown* decision, which fundamentally reshaped the American legal, political, and social landscape.

Brown, perhaps more than any Supreme Court case in history, highlighted the potentially revolutionary role of the judiciary in setting the boundaries of public life, and it revived old debates about the proper relation of federal to state power. Moreover, *Brown* forced America as a nation and Americans as individuals to confront and reckon with values, beliefs, and impulses that were sharply dividing, ranging from the role of the judiciary to definitions of equality to the nation's capacity to live up to its professed core beliefs.[25]

Affirmative action policies have undisputedly advanced opportunity for Black Americans and other racial minorities, who now occupy senior chairs in many of our most prestigious and influential institutions from the Supreme Court to university presidencies, corporate boardrooms, and the highest echelons of government. But this is not an argument for the end of such policies, especially in the realm of education. Quite the opposite.

As we will argue, now is the time for leaders in higher education to advocate—robustly and publicly—in defense of affirmative action in the interest of civic equality. The "diversity" rationale, which has defined and delimited our discussions and thinking about affirmative action since Justice Powell's opinion in *Bakke,* is not without validity. But it should not divert our attention away from the core reason for these policies, which is the necessity of coming to terms with a history of invidious discrimination—one uniquely affecting Black Americans (and then extending to other historically disadvantaged groups).

The trajectory of Black Americans' lives in the years to come will be shaped by the Supreme Court when it hears two separate affirmative action cases in the 2022–2023 term: *Students for Fair Admissions v. Harvard* and *Students for Fair Admissions v. University of North Carolina at Chapel Hill.* The first case, filed against Harvard University, contends that the university's race-conscious admissions policy discriminates against Asian American applicants in violation of Title VI of the Civil Rights Act of 1964.[26] The second case alleges that UNC unconstitutionally favors Black and Hispanic students over others (including Asian American and white students).[27]

As affirmative action faces its gravest threat in a generation, we assert that the time has come to reappraise the Fourteenth Amendment rationale of what equal protection under the law *really* means, and should mean. In the decades following the *Brown* decision, the nation soon discovered that not discriminating against Black citizens going forward was not enough to mitigate a centuries-long history of severe injustice, a "legacy of discrimination," as Justice Thurgood Marshall called it.[28] *Brown* may have initiated the end of explicit state-sanctioned discrimination, but the nation had had limited experience with and even less imagination about what the creation of a fairer, or fair, nation might actually look like or entail. This led to the affirmative action policies that followed and the enduring passions they continue to spark to this day.

As debates about affirmative action are waged in the coming decade—in state legislatures, at the ballot box, in classrooms and courtrooms, in the media, and at the kitchen table—America is now presented with a once-in-a-generation opportunity to reassert its commitment to advancing opportunity, dignity, and equality for all Americans, now and for generations to come. Conscience and jurisprudence, we insist, cannot and must not be decoupled.

The Long Journey to
Affirmative Action

Approximately 84 percent of the current U.S. population—more than 281 million people—were born after 1954, when the *Brown vs. Board of Education of Topeka* ruling was issued.[1] Accordingly, more than eight in ten Americans—most readers of this book, along with their relatives, friends, neighbors, schoolmates, and colleagues— have no firsthand memories of state-sanctioned segregation.

Further, even if many, ideally most, of the 281 million Americans born after *Brown* acknowledge that we still have a long way to go on our journey toward racial equity, in a nation that prides itself on its capacity for reinvention, millions of people would prefer not to relitigate or attempt to address the continuing effects of an ugly and embarrassing past.

Yet approximately 16 percent of the U.S. population—about 55 million Americans, the co-authors of this book included among them—were born in the pre-*Brown* era. To that end, we believe it is especially important that readers of this book who were born after *Brown* fully "inhabit" that era. Because, as we explore the social and legal dimensions of affirmative action in the chapters that follow, we posit that many readers, especially white readers, will be shocked to discover what people of color living in this country have always known: That it is foolhardy to believe that the devastating effects of three and a half centuries' worth of systemic racism and discrimination, which began in the early 1600s, could have been reversed and "corrected" as a result of *Brown* and the civil rights legislation of the 1960s, however well-intentioned they were, in the absence of affirmative action.

What we offer here is not original historical research. The scholarship on America and race is monumental and ongoing. We intend to draw on that body of knowledge in order to better understand our subject of affirmative action in the post-*Brown* era in which we are living.

A BRIEF HISTORY OF AMERICAN RACISM FROM RECONSTRUCTION TO *BROWN*

As discussed in the introduction, despite the adoption of the Thirteenth, Fourteenth and Fifteenth Amendments, rulings issued in subsequent Supreme Court cases related to those amendments emboldened white supremacists' efforts to enact "racial purity" laws across the South.[2]

As Eric Foner, author of *Reconstruction: America's Unfinished Journey*, has noted, "You cannot understand America today without understanding this period." Indeed, the divisive issues of the Reconstruction era will be eerily familiar to observers of present-day America, which is still grappling over questions such as *Who is a citizen? Who gets to vote? What is the proper balance to be achieved between federal and state authority? How do we address the threat of domestic terrorism?*[3]

Laws and ordinances—hundreds of them—enacted during the era of British colonial rule and, later, after America gained independence, regulated Black Americans' conduct, denied equal access to opportunity, segregated races, and restricted freedom in daily life. The laws began as "slave codes," formulated in the years prior to the American Revolution. After the United States gained its independence, they evolved in the aftermath of the Civil War into "black codes." Enacted in the states of the former Confederacy, these new laws were designed to replace the social controls over Black citizens that had been removed by the Emancipation Proclamation and the Thirteenth Amendment.[4] Jim Crow laws, as discussed in the introduction, were enacted after 1876 and continued to restrict Black Americans' freedom. While most closely associated with the South, Jim Crow laws reached far and wide, from Georgia to Oregon, from Massachusetts to Arizona, and to nearly all points in between.[5]

Then, as now, one of the key areas in which white supremacy was exerted was in policing. While the term *racial profiling* may not have been familiar in 1900, it was common practice, as Black Americans were monitored and harassed by law enforcement officials, subjected to draconian penalties for petty crimes, and incarcerated at much higher rates than were whites. Forced labor schemes allowed Black prisoners to be "rented out" to privately owned companies—from mines to railroads to lumber companies—at submarket rates, which in turn depressed the wages of free Black workers.[6]

Another dimension of the post-Emancipation South: Terror. Mobs claimed the lives of nearly five thousand Black men, women, and children between 1877 and 1950. White people representing every stratum of society participated in the violence, which was either enabled or ignored by law enforcement authorities. When pleas for justice were made before the courts, all-white grand juries refused to indict perpetrators, routinely claiming that Black victims "died at the hands of persons unknown."[7] The abhorrent actions directed at Black Americans were intended in part to inculcate docility in, and deny dignity to, Black citizens. Less visible, though, was the extent to which these actions ensured that Black persons could not ascend economically. Qualitatively, more than three centuries of racial violence and discrimination helped shape a broader, toxic national context which ensured that Black Americans were "kept down."

One of the Supreme Court's most important decisions in this era was *Plessy v. Ferguson*.[8] In 1890, the state of Louisiana passed the Separate Car Act, which required racially segregated accommodations for Black and white passengers on railroads, including separate railway cars. Such racial segregation was commonplace at the time.

A group of prominent Black, creole of color, and white creole New Orleans residents banded together to challenge the law. In 1892 they persuaded Homer Plessy, whose ancestry was seven-eighths white and one-eighth Black, to test the law. Plessy, who under the law was classified as Black, bought a first-class ticket in New Orleans and boarded a train bound for Covington, Louisiana. After he took a seat in a whites-only railway car, Plessy was asked to relocate to the Blacks-only car. Plessy refused and was arrested. He challenged the constitutionality of the law. The case ascended to the Supreme Court of the United States in 1896. In that landmark case, the Court, in an eight-to-one decision, ruled that "separate," but ostensibly "equal," facilities for Black and white Americans did not violate the Fourteenth Amendment's guarantee of equal protection under the law to all American citizens.[9]

By the turn of the century, the emergence of Jim Crow laws drove the final stake through the heart of Reconstruction. "Reconstruction marked the lowest point in the saga of American Democracy," observed Foner. "Most historians view Reconstruction as a tragedy. The tragedy was not that it had been attempted, but that it failed."[10]

In 1917, when the United States entered World War I, President Woodrow Wilson justified America's intervention as a means to advance democracy and protect liberalism and individual freedom. Interpreting this as a welcome signal that what America preached abroad might compel the nation finally to embrace the same values at home, NAACP founding leader W. E. B. Du Bois wrote, "From now on we may expect to see the walls of prejudice gradually crumble before the onslaught of common sense and social progress."[11] Sadly, the double standard endured: 350,000 undersupplied, overdisciplined Black soldiers were shipped off to Europe under strict Jim Crow conditions under the command of white officers, some of whom occasionally shot Black troops. Upon their re-entry at the war's end, many Black veterans became politically active, resolving to aggressively push back against Jim Crow.

Another effect of the war: Black out-migration from the South sparked by wartime labor shortages in the North increased dramatically throughout the 1920s. This great migration north of the Mason-Dixon line would become a mass social movement—six million Black Americans would migrate north by 1970.[12] On their arrival, they may have been welcomed by whites as laborers, but not as neighbors or prospective classmates for their children. As these discriminatory policies of towns and municipalities steered Black people into the most undesirable urban areas, dispatched their children to substandard segregated schools, and denied them access to well-paid jobs, the summer of 1919 sparked racial violence in Chicago and Washington, DC, among other cities. The violence, most of it white-on-Black, was so extreme that one NAACP leader dubbed it the "Red Summer."[13]

* * *

At the same time migratory patterns were shifting, so, too, were po-litical winds within the Democratic Party. Staunchly segregationist during the first half of the twentieth century, party loyalists, espe-cially in the South, shrewdly reelected their federal representatives again and again, allowing Democrats to amass seniority and wield outsized influence over congressional lawmaking and resource allo-cation. Accordingly, when New Deal legislation sought to distribute Social Security benefits, Democrats ensured that agricultural and domestic laborers, two-thirds of the southern Black labor force, were excluded; when anti-lynching legislation was introduced, it was blocked. But by the late 1930s, Black voters residing in the North and the West—voters whose presence in those regions had expanded substantially since the Great Migration—began to be ab-sorbed into the Democratic Party. It would take decades, but, even-tually, the party with a shamefully racist legacy would emerge as the architect of the most sweeping civil rights legislation in the nation's history.[14]

Eleven months before the outbreak of World War II, in his annual State of the Union Address, President Franklin Roosevelt, making the case for America's continued support of its ally Great Britain, invoked four universal freedoms worthy of America's defense: freedom of speech, freedom of worship, freedom from want, and freedom from fear.[15] After America entered the war and sixteen mil-lion Americans, Black and white, joined the war effort, Black leaders added a fifth freedom to President Roosevelt's list: freedom from ra-cial segregation. The Black press dubbed this call for a fifth freedom the "Double V" campaign—for victory at home and abroad.[16] And at home, Black civil rights proponents were aided in that effort by the Supreme Court in *Smith v. Allwright*, which ruled that the South's system of racially restrictive primary elections violated the

Fifteenth Amendment[17] An estimated six hundred thousand Black southerners registered to vote in 1946, triple the number in 1940.

Indeed, there were promising signs that the positive momentum for Black Americans would continue through the second half of the 1940s, especially when the Servicemen's Readjustment Act of 1944, known popularly as the GI Bill of Rights, was signed into law. Designed to reintegrate millions of returning soldiers into the postwar American economy and society, the GI Bill sought to give veterans a leg up once they were home. Under the provisions of the bill, the United States Employment Service would place unskilled laborers in jobs; college tuition assistance would ostensibly propel millions of first-generation college and university students into the professions; small business loans would assist budding entrepreneurs; and federally guaranteed low-interest mortgages would facilitate first-time home ownership.[18] Sadly, and predictably, Black veterans were shortchanged: The United States Employment Service discriminated when it came to job placements, especially in the South.[19] Black aspirants to (segregated) higher education had far fewer colleges and universities to choose from. And most of the historically Black colleges and universities were geographically concentrated in the South, far from many returning veterans' homes, which may explain, in part, why in the years following the war, the gap in educational achievement between Black and white Americans actually widened instead of narrowing.

When it came to housing benefits, one provision of the bill called for offering low-interest, zero-down-payment home loans to servicemen, with more favorable terms for new construction than for existing housing.[20] While these policies were designed to be race-neutral in principle, in practice they disproportionately helped white men just as they had in the past.[21] Redlining—the systemic practice of excluding Black homeowners from mortgage lending—was endemic in the years following the passage of the 1934 National Housing Act during the Great Depression: More than $116 billion of an approved $120 billion (more than 98 percent) in federally backed mortgages approved between 1938 and 1962 went to white homeowners.[22] In the unlikely event that Black buyers *could* secure a loan, they were forced into higher-rate loans and required to live in majority-Black areas within the community, where real estate assets were less likely to appreciate relative to those in majority-white communities. Our colleague Ira Katznelson summarized these powerful pieces of social legislation as, in effect, the equivalent of a Marshall Plan for white Americans.[23]

By the late 1940s, tensions within the Democratic party heightened. In 1947, with an address to the NAACP's annual conference as the backdrop, President Harry Truman announced the formation of the President's Commission on Civil Rights. The launch of this initiative sent a strong signal to the world—as well as to the segregationist southern wing of his party. In what amounted to an unambiguous assault on Jim Crow, Truman proclaimed that, in America, "there is no justifiable reason for discrimination because of ancestry, or religion, or race, or color. Every man should have the right to a decent home, the right to an education, the right to adequate medical care, the right to a worthwhile job, the right to an equal share in making the public decisions through the ballot, and the right to a fair trial in court."[24] A year later, Truman laid out a ten-point legislative agenda to secure those rights. He also issued executive orders prohibiting discrimination in federal employment and ending segregation in the armed forces. Southern Democrats took notice. Then they took action. At the 1948 Democratic National Convention, thirty-five delegates from Alabama and Mississippi stormed out of the convention and formed the National States'

Rights Party. The Dixiecrats, as they were known, then nominated South Carolina governor Strom Thurmond for president.[25]

But while southern Democrats may have disliked the direction in which their country was headed, the Black diaspora that had migrated from the South to the Midwest and the West felt differently, and their votes in the 1948 presidential election—especially in pivotal states such as California, Illinois, and Ohio—helped nudge Truman over the finish line.

But, yet again, as weary Black Americans had since the end of the Civil War been made acutely aware, the gap between what America claimed it owed Black Americans and what it actually delivered to them remained frustratingly wide: The Eighty-First Congress, convened in January 1949, a Congress that included only 2 black congressmen (out of 435) and no Black senators,[26] rejected Truman's civil rights initiatives.[27]

It bears repeating that there is, of course, a vast and ever-deepening literature on the subject of invidious discrimination against Black Americans. We make no pretense of providing either a novel or comprehensive history of such discrimination. What we strive to do here—and throughout this book—is to engage with our shared national history of inequality and injustice involving race in ways that *must* shape our understanding of our Constitution today.

Thus, as the 1940s turned the corner into the 1950s, the lived experience of Black Americans remained in stasis. This group accounted for 10 percent of the population. But that did not translate into access to 10 percent of the nation's spoils. They were underrepresented not only in Congress, but across federal, state, and local governments. No Black justice sat on the Supreme Court, no Black person served as a governor, and in an era when suppression of the Black vote was commonplace, no major U.S. cities were led by a Black mayor.[28] Black Americans were still denied housing.

Black Americans were still denied jobs and career advancement opportunities: The percentage of Black men engaged in nonmanual, white-collar work numbered in the mid-single digits, while the overwhelming majority worked in manual jobs. In the South, Black men were overrepresented in agricultural labor. In industrial settings, most Black workers were still denied promotions.[29] Black women worked, primarily, as domestic servants—often working twelve-hour shifts for paltry wages.[30] Entrepreneurship, in theory, could have been a path toward upward mobility, but Black entrepreneurs keen to start a small business were denied capital.[31] And friends and family, if they were Black, were not likely to have investable cash given that, in the 1950s, the median annual income of Black families was barely half the average for white families.[32] And, of course, in states across the nation, but especially in the South, Black children were prohibited from attending school with white children.

By mid-century, the lived experience of Black Americans—particularly their increasing anger and frustration with the status quo, coupled with the yearning for equality—was voiced potently in a poem called "Democracy," published in 1949 by Langston Hughes:

> I tire so of hearing people say,
> Let things take their course.
> Tomorrow is another day.
> I do not need my freedom when I'm dead.
> I cannot live on tomorrow's bread.
> . . . I live here, too.
> I want my freedom
> Just as you.[33]

BROWN AND ITS AFTERMATH

In 1953, President Dwight Eisenhower appointed California's governor, Earl Warren, Chief Justice of the Supreme Court. The new Chief Justice was thrust immediately into the most incendiary issue in American politics: the race question. Five separate NAACP-sponsored school desegregation cases, all of them calling into question the validity of *Plessy v. Ferguson,* awaited him on his arrival in Washington.[34]

With regard to the matter of race, the Court was divided between those who found segregation abhorrent and those who were reticent about inciting a social revolution in the South. Chief Justice Warren, who had for three terms served as governor of one of America's most diverse states, knew where he wanted the Court to land, but he was also shrewd enough to realize he would have to find judicial common ground if he were to achieve a unanimous opinion.[35]

The opinion in *Brown v. Board of Education of Topeka, Kansas,* which centered on ten-year-old Linda Brown, was issued on May 17, 1954.[36] The unanimous ruling did not mince words: "In the field of public education the [*Plessy*] doctrine of 'separate but equal' has no place. Separate educational facilities are inherently unequal." A follow-up decision in 1955, known as *Brown II,* ushered in the implementation phase of school desegregation. Local authorities nationwide were instructed to move with "all deliberate speed" to desegregate public schools.[37]

Seven decades on, the *Brown* decision has become so iconic that it is easy to overlook the jurisprudential advantage enjoyed by segregation's defenders in 1954. By any reckoning, precedent was

on the side of the South. Of the forty-four challenges to school segregation mounted between 1865 and 1935, none had succeeded.

But the Court had begun chipping away at the notion of "separate
but equal" accommodation within twenty years of the *Plessy* decision, beginning in 1914 with *McCabe v. Atchison, Topeka and Santa
Fe Railway*.[38] In *McCabe*, the Court upheld the argument that rail-
road companies that provided first-class cars for white people had
to do the same for Black passengers. Three years later, in *Buchanan
v. Warley*, the Court rejected Louisville's "residential checkerboard
law," which segregated neighborhoods block by block, as an unconstitutional limit on individual property rights.[39] In 1938, in *Gaines
v. Canada*, the Court, drawing on *McCabe*, ruled that a law that
forced Black, but not white, residents of Missouri to leave the state
to obtain a legal education violated the Equal Protection Clause.[40]
In 1950, in *Sweatt v. Painter*, the Court ruled that a "separate but
equal" law school established for Black Texans was unconstitutional because it was inferior to the (all-white) University of Texas
Law School.[41] In *McLauren v. Oklahoma State Board of Regents*, also
decided in 1950, the Court held that Oklahoma had violated the
Equal Protection Clause when it required a Black student admitted
to the University of Oklahoma Law School to sit at a special table
in the cafeteria, a designated desk in the school library, and a desk
outside the classroom doorway[42] As a result of these decisions, the
Court had clearly established that "equal" meant "equal," even if
separate.

But the Court had still not yet held that separation on the
basis of race was itself a violation of the Equal Protection Clause.
Indeed, several of the Justices who had voted in favor of Sweatt
and McLaurin were keen to maintain the status quo, among them
Justice Stanley Reed, a Kentuckian, who argued that segregation
protected people against "the mixing of races." The preservation

of "racial purity," then, was a legitimate state interest—so long as "equal" meant "equal."

Then came *Brown v. Board of Education*, wherein the NAACP lawyers who brought the case maintained that segregation was inherently unequal and therefore unconstitutional. At that time, the Supreme Court was "fractured along personal and political lines . . . [and] divided . . . between those who considered segregation 'Hitler's creed' (in the words of Justice Robert Jackson, who had prosecuted leading Nazis at the Nuremberg Trials after WWII) and those who were unprepared to impose a social revolution on the South."[43] Warren, an eminently patient and polite Chief Justice who was also highly attuned to the popular support for segregation, "worked assiduously to find judicial common ground fertile enough to achieve a unanimous opinion."[44]

In the *Brown* opinion, authored by Warren, the Court agreed, holding that "to separate" Black children "from others . . . solely because of their race generates a feeling of inferiority as to their status in the community that may affect their hearts and minds in a way unlikely ever to be undone. . . . Whatever may have been the extent of psychological knowledge at the time of *Plessy*, this finding is amply supported by modern authority. Any language in *Plessy* to the contrary to this finding is rejected." School segregation, the Court concluded, was not innocuous but harmful, and the reason for imposing it was not neutral but discriminatory.

In the decision, Chief Justice Warren elaborated:

> Today, education is perhaps the most important function of state and local governments. Compulsory school attendance laws and the great expenditures for education both demonstrate our recognition of the importance of education to our democratic society. It is required in the performance of our most basic public

responsibilities, even service in the armed forces. It is the very foundation of good citizenship. Today it is a principal instrument in awakening the child to cultural values, in preparing him for later professional training, and in helping him to adjust normally to his environment. In these days, it is doubtful that any child may reasonably be expected to succeed in life if he is denied the opportunity of an education. Such an opportunity, where the state has undertaken to provide it, is a right which must be made available to all on equal terms.[45]

Warren continued:

Segregation of white and colored children in public schools has a detrimental effect upon the colored children. The impact is greater when it has the sanction of the law; for the policy of separating the races is usually interpreted as denoting the inferiority of the negro group. A sense of inferiority affects the motivation of a child to learn. Segregation with the sanction of law, therefore, has a tendency to (retard) the educational and mental development of Negro children and to deprive them of some of the benefits they would receive in a racial(ly) integrated school system.[46]

Announcing the *Brown* decision was one thing. Enforcing it was another. And both the Court and the NAACP underestimated the determination of white southerners to reject the decision and to maintain segregation. After *Brown*, desegregation proceeded largely without incident in the North and the West,[47] but in the South, those who were keen to frustrate desegregation efforts identified minor enforcement loopholes in *Brown II*—and pounced. And the southerners who were less skilled, or perhaps uninterested, in the art of legal hair-splitting simply declared war on the Court. The South, bellowed Mississippi senator James Eastland, would not "abide by or obey this legislative decision by a political court."[48]

Thus, in early 1956, roughly 80 percent of the members of the South's congressional delegation signed the "Southern Manifesto," which denounced the *Brown* decision as a "clear abuse of judicial power." The manifesto called on white southerners to "resist forced integration by any lawful means."[49]

Millions of white citizens across the South readily complied, enthusiastically accepting Virginia Democratic senator Harry Byrd's invitation to put up a "massive resistance" to integration. The battle was under way: Virginia closed public schools rather than desegregate them; Confederate battle flags, last seen waving outside a state capitol building almost a century earlier, suddenly reappeared in South Carolina and Alabama; and Mississippi and several other states abolished mandatory school attendance laws, leaving classrooms mostly empty—except for Black students.[50]

In September 1957, President Eisenhower signed into law the first federal civil rights legislation since Reconstruction: the 1957 Civil Rights Act. Passage of this law was not the big civil rights story that fall, though. That honor went to Central High School in Little Rock, Arkansas, where nine African American students were welcomed to the otherwise all-white school by a threatening mob dedicated to the preservation of white racial purity through resistance to enforcement of the *Brown* decision. The mob, in turn, was greeted by the 101st Airborne Division, which was dispatched, reluctantly, by the nation's commander-in-chief when it became clear that Arkansas governor Orval E. Faubus did not intend to uphold the law. In what would become one of the most iconic images of the civil rights era, newspapers across the nation published photographs of sixteen-year-old Minnijean Brown, one of the nine Black children, being escorted into Central High. "For the first time in my life I feel like an American citizen," she said.[51] That evening, the president, who had distanced himself from the decision, addressed the American people on television, saying "Our personal opinions about the decision have no bearing on the matter of enforcement; the responsibility and authority of the Supreme Court to interpret the Constitution are very clear." It was the duty of Americans, he said, to demonstrate "to the world that we are a nation in which laws, not men, are supreme."[52]

* * *

In their decisions, the Supreme Court Justices were exceedingly careful in how they chose and parsed their words. When the directive to use "all deliberate speed" was issued in *Brown II* by the same jurists who had ruled in *Brown* the directive was interpreted by some observers as a retreat from—and perhaps even a betrayal of—*Brown*'s original promise. Was the Court talking about fully integrating schools in weeks? Months? Years? When asked his opinion, Thurgood Marshall, who had argued *Brown* before the Supreme Court, said he believed the Court's opinion in *Brown II* was coded language for "S-L-O-W."[53] If *Brown* qualified as a cause for celebration, decades later some retrospective appraisals of *Brown II* described it as a "cause for despair."[54]

This concern that too much change too soon, regardless of how long it is overdue, might create a severe backlash among the white southern majority, informed jurists' thinking both in the 1950s and in subsequent decades.

RESISTANCE TO THE CIVIL RIGHTS MOVEMENT

Before *Brown*, civil rights activism was concentrated primarily in northern and western cities that had sizable Black populations. As the 1950s turned the corner into the 1960s, it was time to take the movement to the South. A diverse coalition of civil rights activists resolved to deploy a variety of nonviolent direct-action tactics— boycotts, picketing, marches, and sit-ins—to accelerate integration across the South. Thus, in 1961 an integrated group of workers from the Congress of Racial Equality embarked on a "freedom ride" through the South to test a recent Supreme Court decision that prohibited racial segregation in facilities involved in interstate travel. On their arrival in Alabama, the freedom riders were mauled by violent mobs in Anniston, Birmingham, and most infamously, Montgomery.[55]

The Kennedy administration, which had taken office less than four months before this violence, and which, like the administration that preceded it, was reluctant to wade too deeply into the most polarizing domestic issue confronting the nation, was provoked into action, just as the Congress of Racial Equality had hoped. In response to the violence in Alabama, Attorney General Robert Kennedy instructed the Interstate Commerce Commission to ban segregation and discrimination in interstate travel. But any hopes he may have harbored that his order to the commission would appease activists and encourage them to stand down were dashed as another civil rights group, the Student Nonviolent Coordinating Committee (SNCC), launched a voter registration campaign in Mississippi, where only 5 percent of eligible Black voters were registered.[56]

The SNCC believed (rightly, as it turned out), that a voter registration drive in the Deep South would provoke an even more vitriolic response from local white people than the freedom rides had. Only a month into their campaign, four Black churches used as voter registration sites were firebombed; SNCC workers in Mississippi were arrested and beaten; and Black residents were terrorized, among them Herbert Lee, a farmer and World War II veteran with civic ambitions who was shot and killed by a white Mississippi state legislator.[57]

In September 1962, like Eisenhower before him, President Kennedy authorized the use of military power after efforts to integrate the University of Mississippi degenerated into a riot that resulted in two deaths. Then, in May 1963, Reverend Martin Luther King Jr. of the Southern Christian Leadership Conference led a group to Birmingham, where the commissioner of public safety, Eugene "Bull" Connor—in what would become one of the most grotesque displays of government "resistance" during the civil rights era—attacked young Black men and women with batons, immobilized marchers with high-pressure fire hoses, and set German shepherd police dogs on the activists. The images, splashed across newspaper front pages and television screens worldwide, shocked observers and humiliated the United States abroad.[58]

The Kennedy bothers, despite their best efforts to stay out of the fray, finally sided decisively with the civil rights movement after Alabama governor George Wallace, in his 1963 inaugural address, called for "segregation now, segregation tomorrow, segregation forever."[59] What some, especially in the South, had hoped—that the issue could be framed as a dispute over federal authority versus states' rights—was definitively challenged in a June 12, 1963, speech delivered by John Kennedy, broadcast live on radio and television. In his remarks the president cast the civil rights struggle as a moral issue "as old as the scriptures and . . . as clear as the American

Constitution." The time had come, he declared, for the nation to "fulfill its promise."[60]

Shortly after the conclusion of Kennedy's speech, Mississippi NAACP leader Medgar Evers pulled into his driveway, stepped out of his car, and was felled by an assassin's bullet.

Unleashing yet another round of moral outrage, the civil rights movement, which historian C. Vann Woodward dubbed "The Second Reconstruction,"[61] would now gain even greater momentum and accelerate concurrently on two parallel tracks, the political and the social. Congress drafted new legislation designed to expand voting rights, hasten school desegregation, integrate public facilities, and compel local compliance with federal laws. On the social front, in August 1963, 250,000 people gathered on the National Mall in Washington, DC, to hear Martin Luther King Jr.'s "I Have a Dream" speech, which became a rallying cry for liberation movements worldwide and transformed the civil rights leader into an international icon.[62]

After President Kennedy's assassination in Dallas on November 22, 1963, his successor, Lyndon B. Johnson, pushed the 1964 Civil Rights Act through Congress. A southerner himself, Johnson was keenly aware that the struggle for civil rights was not only a moral issue, but an economic one as well. Accordingly, he launched a series of social welfare programs that would come to be known as "the Great Society."

The South remained recalcitrant and "resistance" persisted. After a massive voter registration drive orchestrated by college-age SNCC volunteers was launched in Mississippi in 1964, the effort was greeted by unprecedented violence and intimidation at the hands of local police and the Ku Klux Klan. Thirty-five churches were burned to the ground that summer, and six people were murdered, compelling President Johnson to call on Congress to up the ante even further and enact the Voting Rights Act of 1965, which banned literacy tests and allowed the federal government to oversee elections in counties in which less than 50 percent of the population had voted in the 1964 presidential election.[63]

FIRST AMENDMENT BATTLES OVER CIVIL RIGHTS

Civil rights battles also played out in the courts. As the struggle on the streets heated up, southern state legislators waged a sustained legal assault to limit the speech of Black ministers, thwart protesters from assembling, prevent civil rights advocates from litigating, and chill press reporting on race, resulting in several landmark First Amendment rulings. From 1958 to 1969 about a dozen First Amendment cases ascended to the Supreme Court. Together they helped shape the modern conception of free speech and a free press, one which lasts to this day. This emerging body of law in an area of such fundamental importance to our nation demonstrates what all scholars of constitutional law know: that *Brown* had transformative and radiating consequences throughout our system of government and in the American psyche.

Three of the cases blunted governmental attempts reminiscent of the McCarthy era a decade earlier to compel the NAACP to disclose the names of the organization's supporters. Given the state of affairs in Alabama, the effect of these laws was to deter anyone from supporting the NAACP. In *NAACP v. Alabama* (1958), the Court unanimously held that an order requiring the NAACP to produce records, including the names and addresses of all members and agents, was an impermissible restraint on members' exercise of their right to freedom of association.[64] Similarly, in *Bates v. City of Little Rock* (1960), the Court held that the City of Little Rock could not constitutionally require the compulsory disclosure of the membership lists of the local branches of the NAACP, finding that such disclosure "would work a significant interference with the freedom of association of their members."[65] After a local chapter of the NAACP in Florida refused to turn over membership records to a legislative committee—ostensibly to determine whether the NAACP's members were communists—the civil rights organization was convicted of contempt. The Supreme Court, in *Gibson v. Fla. Legislative Investigation Comm.* (1963), held that the conviction was unsupported by evidence. Although the committee was empowered to investigate "subversive and Communist activities," the Court held that it had failed to show a substantial connection between local NAACP and Communist activities.[66]

Across the South, state actors routinely sought to intimidate peaceful protestors into silence. In *Garner v. Louisiana* (1961), the Court voided convictions under a Louisiana "breach of the peace" statute that was used to stop peaceful sit-in demonstrations, holding that the evidence was insufficient to support a finding that defendants, by sitting at "white lunch counters," disturbed the peace either by outwardly boisterous conduct or by passive conduct.[67] Similarly, the Court in *Edwards v. South Carolina* (1963) voided breach of peace convictions after defendants marched peacefully on a sidewalk around State House grounds to publicize discriminatory government action. In so doing, the Court held that these convictions violated defendants' constitutionally protected rights of free speech, free assembly, and freedom to petition for redress of grievances.[68]

Two years later, in *Cox v. Louisiana* (1965), the Court held that the conviction of a defendant who led a group of students to protest the arrests of civil rights advocates was unconstitutional. The state statute, construed as allowing people to be punished merely for peacefully expressing unpopular views, violated the constitutional right of free speech and assembly.[69] Stubborn Louisiana, which must have appeared to Supreme Court Justices as incapable of accepting "no" for an answer, continued to violate the constitutional rights of civil rights advocates. In *Brown v. Louisiana* (1966), the Court held, for the fourth time in five years, that breach the of peace convictions of defendants who staged a peaceful sit-in at a segregated public library could not stand, because such action constitutes protected symbolic speech.[70] The Court likewise affirmed the rights of peaceful protestors in 1969's *Gregory v. City of Chicago* and *Shuttlesworth v. Birmingham*.[71]

Thurgood Marshall, arguing once again on behalf of the NAACP, appeared before the high court in *NAACP v. Button* (1963) to challenge a state law in Virginia designed to prevent prospective plaintiffs from seeking legal counsel. The statute precluded groups or third-party entities from advising individuals that their legal rights had been infringed and refer such victims to another attorney or organization. In its decision, the Supreme Court protected the First Amendment rights of a civil rights group to engage in public interest litigation.[72]

These cases were all crucial to protecting and advancing the First Amendment rights of civil rights advocates in the 1960s, but the Supreme Court ruling that had the broadest and most influential effect was *New York Times v. Sullivan*. This landmark 1964 decision reversed a judgment for libel damages against the *New York Times*, expanding and protecting the rights of news organizations and publishers to criticize government officials. Prior to the case, journalists who dared criticize government leaders faced the threat of a libel lawsuit, an intimidation tactic that, for decades, effectively chilled many journalists' speech.

The facts of the case are as follows: On March 29, 1960, the *New York Times* published an advertisement titled "Heed Their Rising Voices." A fundraising appeal, the advertisement established a legal defense fund for Martin Luther King Jr., who was routinely arrested and harassed by police and other governmental authorities in various states across the South. The newspaper ad asserted that King had been arrested seven times "for 'speeding,' 'loitering,' and similar 'offenses.'" Further, the advertisement continued, "In Montgomery, Alabama, after students sang 'My Country, 'Tis of Thee' on the State Capitol steps, their leaders were expelled from school, and truck-loads of police armed with shotguns and tear-gas ringed the Alabama State College Campus. When the entire student body protested to state authorities by refusing to re-register, their dining hall was pad-locked in an attempt to starve them into submission."[73]

After viewing the advertisement, L. B. Sullivan, the city commissioner in Montgomery who oversaw the local police, sued the *New York Times*, claiming that the ad was factually inaccurate and harmed his reputation. A local jury agreed and awarded him $500,000 in damages. The goal of such a large damage award was not to compensate Sullivan for the "harms" he suffered but, rather, to drive northern media away from covering the suppression of civil rights protesters in the South. When, four years later, the Supreme Court issued its ruling in the case, Justice William J. Brennan Jr., writing for the majority, stated that "debate on public issues should be uninhibited, robust and wide-open."[74] The Court acknowledged that there were indeed some factual errors in the *Times* ad: For example, King had been arrested four times, not seven. And some of the details about the protest at Alabama State College were inaccurate. But those errors were acceptable, the Court said. Intense criticism, as well as occasional factual errors, were the price a democratic society had to pay to ensure freedom.

In its ruling, the Supreme Court decreed that public officials must meet a higher standard for libel judgments than ordinary private citizens. In order to win a libel case, the plaintiff had to demonstrate that a news outlet *deliberately or recklessly* published false information. Thus was established the "actual malice" standard, whereupon a public official keen to sue for libel had to prove that demonstrably inaccurate statements about his or her professional conduct or personal character were made "with knowledge that it was false or with reckless disregard of whether it was false or not." The Court held that the plaintiff had not proved that the *Times* advertisement was published with actual malice.[75] It is no exaggeration to say that this case accelerated the two major protest movements of the 1960s, the civil rights movement and the movement against the Vietnam War.

ECONOMIC AND EDUCATIONAL ASPECTS OF RACIAL INEQUALITY

While *Brown* and the civil rights movement unfolded as a major social, political, and moral conflict, there was another important dimension to the story: Black Americans' quest for upward economic mobility. In his first State of the Union speech, in January 1964, President Johnson announced a "war on poverty." The new president, one of the most masterful legislators ever to serve in Congress, was determined to transform his rhetoric into action. At the center of his legislative agenda was the Economic Opportunity Act of 1964, pursuant to which the newly formed Office of Economic Opportunity was tasked with delivering job skills training to non-college-bound workers. His Revenue Act of 1964 cut taxes to stimulate economic growth and job creation; the Food Stamp Act of 1964 ensured that individuals and families living below the poverty line would be nourished.[76] Mindful that perhaps the most reliable path up from poverty was education, the president—a former schoolteacher—championed the Elementary and Secondary Education Act, which directed federal money to local public schools. The Head Start program readied children of the poor for kindergarten. The Higher Education Act provided students with access to low-interest federal loans.[77]

Four months after introducing his "Great Society" initiatives, during a commencement address at the University of Michigan, the president elucidated his vision further. A Great Society, he said, is one that "rests on abundance and liberty for all. It demands an end to poverty and racial injustice.... The Great Society is a place where every child can find knowledge to enrich his mind and to enlarge his talents.... It is a place where the city of man serves not only the needs of the body and the demand of commerce but the desire for beauty and the hunger for community."[78]

One year after his speech at the University of Michigan, President Johnson addressed the graduates of historically Black Howard University. With the Civil Rights Act of 1964 and the Voting Rights Act of 1965 expected to arrive on his desk to be signed into law in only a matter of days, Johnson was upbeat about the progress he had driven, but not yet prepared to declare an end to the nation's civil rights journey. In remarks that may have unintentionally anticipated the battles over affirmative action that would come to the fore in the late 1970s and stubbornly re-assert themselves during the four decades that followed, he insisted, "You do not wipe away the scars of centuries by saying: 'Now you are free to go where you want, and do as you desire, and choose the leaders you please.' You do not take a person who, for years, has been hobbled by chains and liberate him, bring him up to the starting line of a race and then say, 'You are free to compete with all the others,' and still justly believe that you have been completely fair." All Americans, Johnson said, "seek not just . . . equality as a right and a theory but equality as a fact and equality as a result. . . . Equal opportunity is essential, but not enough, not enough." Equal treatment in the present could not address the current effects of severe inequality in the past.[79]

The Great Society lifted millions of Americans, Black and white, out of poverty. In 1960, two in ten Americans were classified as poor. By the decade's end, that number had fallen to about one in ten. Black Americans' progress, however, was slower: In 1960 more than five in ten lived below the poverty line; by 1968 the number had dropped to about three in ten.[80]

Black Americans still had a lot of economic catching up to do.

Title VII of the Civil Rights Act of 1964 prohibited discrimination in employment for reasons of race, color, sex, religion, and national origin. And after the civil rights legislation was enacted and employers faced the threat of litigation for noncompliance, the share of Black employees in workplaces increased. But too many Black Americans—still relegated to under-resourced neighborhoods and inferior schools, still restricted in their access to job opportunities and the capital essential to building intergenerational wealth—were still unable to equally access the American Dream's promise of economic mobility. Accordingly, in 1968, Martin Luther King Jr. planned a new march on Washington, this one called a "Poor People's Campaign," to plead the Black community's case for economic justice.[81] Like Johnson, King believed that true equality remained impossible until economic security was fully enjoyed by people of all racial backgrounds. The organizers had an explicitly economic understanding of the costs of segregation, and the campaign was intended to protest the "high levels of black unemployment, work that offered most African Americans only minimal wages and poor job mobility, systematic disenfranchisement of many African Americans, and the persistence of racial segregation in the South."[82] The Poor People's Campaign was still in the planning stages when King was assassinated in Memphis on April 4, 1968. Ten weeks later, the march took place, led by King's Southern Christian Leadership Conference mentor, colleague, and friend, Ralph Abernathy.[83]

As the 1960s wound down, friction between those who believed the nation was not doing enough to redress the enduring effects of past and ongoing racial discrimination and those who believed the nation had fulfilled its obligation to Black Americans continued. And the friction within the Democratic Party between civil rights advocates at the federal level and civil rights resisters in the South had reached a boiling point, as southern Democratic leaders and voters felt increasingly marginalized within their party. Scores of white southern voters were defecting from the Democratic Party and becoming Republicans.

This trend did not go unnoticed. In 1968 Republican presidential nominee Richard Nixon, who shrewdly assessed the mood and struck. Mindful that the South could tip the electoral scales in his favor, he calibrated his pitch to white voters: His GOP platform promised a restoration of order in response to an extraordinarily turbulent year, when the country was stunned by the assassinations of Martin Luther King Jr. and Robert F. Kennedy and shocked by student protests at the Democratic National Convention in Chicago.[84] Nixon sensed—and exploited—many Americans' fatigue with social and political uproar. Appealing to what he called the "Silent Majority," Nixon invited voters to defend the homeland against "attacks on traditional values."

In order to help him win over electoral rival George Wallace's constituency, Nixon relied on the endorsement of former Dixiecrat and recent Republican convert Strom Thurmond, one of the

Senate's most avowed segregationists.[85] Thurmond's support was instrumental to Nixon's general election triumph in 1968, and it has since come to light that Nixon won over Thurmond with promises to use a light presidential touch in enforcing school desegregation.[86]

After he won the presidency, Nixon kept his word to Thurmond. When the subject of school busing—the practice of assigning and transporting students to schools within or outside their local school districts in an effort to diversify the racial makeup of schools— ascended to the top of the national agenda in the early 1970s, the president voiced his opposition to the policy. Adopting white supremacist rhetoric from the 1960s, Nixon declared, "I'm against busing. That's forced integration."[87]

Fifteen years after *Brown*, its desegregation of public schools was now immutable law, and it was complied with by most school districts nationwide—with the exception of various holdouts in the South. Fed up with their foot-dragging, the Supreme Court, now led by Nixon's first appointee, Chief Justice Warren Burger, in *Alexander v. Holmes County Board of Education* (1969), ordered thirty-three school districts in Mississippi to comply with *Brown II*'s "all deliberate speed" provision and desegregate their schools "now."[88] But compelling desegregation was not the same thing as compelling integration, which had no constitutional mandate, as evidenced by the wholesale desertion of public schools for private all-white "segregation academies" and the continuation of dual systems of neighborhood schools, in which the Black neighborhoods of, say, Jackson, Mississippi, retained their Black schools and the more prosperous white communities maintained their white schools.

Busing, which sought to remedy this imbalance, polarized Americans yet again. Many white Americans and indeed, many who supported *Brown* in principle were uneasy when their families' beliefs were put to a firsthand test with busing. It was one thing for

Black students to be bused into majority-white school districts, which were, as a rule, better funded than their Black counterparts. A white parent who fancied him- or herself in step with the times might welcome that. But when it was announced that white children would, reciprocally, be bused into majority-Black school districts, many qualified supporters of integration bristled.

So, too, did some Black parents, who asserted that busing their children from crumbling majority-Black schools and communities to far-away white schools was a false panacea; if the nation was truly committed to uplifting Black America, the better solution was to invest in the economic infrastructures within those communities.[89] That was unlikely to occur. Indeed, when, in the early 1970s, studies showed that 93 percent of Black citizens would have to move in order to achieve integration,[90] policy makers concluded that instead of implementing costly large-scale housing reform, busing students to promote integrated school patterns was a more feasible strategy.[91]

The issue came to a head when, in *Swann v. Charlotte-Mecklenburg Board of Education* (1971), a unanimous Supreme Court endorsed the practice of assigning students to particular schools, even if they were not the closest to their homes, in order to desegregate school districts that intentionally perpetuated segregated schools across district lines.[92] *Swann*, in conjunction with federal denial of education funds to school systems that resisted desegregation efforts, finally broke the back of school segregation in the South.

Not long after the *Swann* decision, President Nixon raised an issue that would inform both the national conversation about, and concomitant legal and public policy and legal reactions to, affirmative action in the decades to come. Nixon distinguished between two types of segregation: de jure and de facto. The former, in his words, were instances "where we have segregation in schools as a result of governmental action." Under this type of state-sanctioned segregation, he asserted, compulsory busing could be deployed to alleviate the problem. But de facto segregation—which was increasingly occurring but was not officially state-sanctioned—was "a result not of what a governmental body did, but a result of housing patterns coming from individual decisions."[93] Nixon thus maintained that, in the absence of de jure segregation, he did not believe that busing to improve the educational opportunities for Black Americans was in the interests of better education.

Nevertheless, by 1973, nearly one in two Black children in the South attended integrated schools, more than anywhere else in America.[94] Indeed, in North Carolina, where *Swann* originated, the busing experiment was viewed as a success, at least in retrospect. Interviewed decades later, Black and white students in Charlotte—now well into middle age—observed that the experience increased their empathy and understanding for one another.[95] Ironically, it was in the North that busing, even after *Swann*, continued to meet resistance. When in 1974 a Detroit judge ordered busing, Mothers Alert Detroit attacked the mandate; in Boston, during that same year, white mobs pelted school buses with bricks and bottles, compelling *Time* to declare busing "the most unpopular institution imposed on Americans since Prohibition."[96]

An emergent generation of state and national politicians—even those far more enlightened than old-guard Dixiecrats—were mindful of how divisive the issue was with voters. When, for example, Joseph Biden of Delaware (a state involved in the original *Brown* ruling) entered the U.S. Senate in 1975, he criticized busing and went so far as to support a constitutional amendment to ban it.[97]

By the mid=1970s, as busing disputes gradually began to wane, a new wave of controversy would soon erupt, this time in higher education. Admissions departments of colleges and universities emerged as the next battleground, in this instance concerning affirmative action. And the case that would establish the framework for considering affirmative action for decades to come was *University of California v. Bakke* (1978).

Affirmative Action

Cases and Policies

During the period between *Brown* and the early 1970s, the nation underwent a profound transition—not only in society, but also on the United States Supreme Court. President John Kennedy seated two Justices on the Court during his brief time in office: Arthur Goldberg, who served only three years before resigning to become the U.S. ambassador to the United Nations, and Byron White, a former deputy attorney general in the Kennedy administration. President Lyndon Johnson, in 1967, appointed Solicitor General Thurgood Marshall, making him the first Black Supreme Court Justice in history.

But President Johnson, who chose not to run for reelection in 1968, ultimately left two seats on the Supreme Court vacant for his successor to fill. Over the following three years, President Richard Nixon appointed four Justices: Chief Justice Warren Burger and Associate Justices William Rehnquist, Harry Blackmun, and Lewis Powell. Accordingly, by the 1970s, the liberal-leaning Warren Court that delivered *Brown* included strong conservative perspectives.

REGENTS OF THE UNIVERSITY OF CALIFORNIA V. BAKKE (1978)

While the key affirmative action case of the 1970s was the *Bakke* decision in 1978, elements of that landmark case were previewed four years earlier in *DeFunis v. Odegaard*. In that case, a white applicant to the University of Washington Law School, Marco DeFunis, was denied entry. A high academic achiever, DeFunis argued that affirmative action was unconstitutional because it favored the admission of minority applicants over "better qualified" white candidates on the basis of race. He successfully petitioned for a mandatory injunction requiring the school to admit him. On appeal, the Washington Supreme Court reversed but allowed DeFunis to remain enrolled until any proceeding in the Supreme Court was resolved. By the time the case reached the Supreme Court, however, DeFunis was just months away from graduation. As a result, the Court ruled that his case was moot.

Though the Court's per curiam opinion did not address the constitutionality of affirmative action, both Justice William Brennan (joined by Justices William O. Douglas, White, and Marshall) and Justice Douglas dissented. In their view the case was not moot, and their dissents addressed the merits. For his part, Justice Douglas argued:

> The Equal Protection Clause did not enact a requirement that law schools employ as the sole criterion for admissions a formula based upon the LSAT and undergraduate grades, nor does it prohibit law schools from evaluating an applicant's prior achievements in light of the barriers that he had to overcome. A black applicant who pulled himself out of the ghetto into a junior

college may thereby demonstrate a level of motivation, perse-
verance, and ability that would lead a fair-minded admissions
committee to conclude that he shows more promise for law
study than the son of a rich alumnus who achieved better grades
at Harvard. That applicant would be offered admission not because he is black, but because as an individual he has shown he
has the potential, while the Harvard man may have taken less advantage of the vastly superior opportunities offered him. Because
of the weight of the prior handicaps, that black applicant may not
realize his full potential in the first year of law school, or even
in the full three years, but in the long pull of a legal career his
achievements may far outstrip those of his classmates whose
earlier records appeared superior by conventional criteria. There
is currently no test available to the Admissions Committee that
can predict such possibilities with assurance, but the Committee
may nevertheless seek to gauge it as best it can and weigh this
factor in its decisions.[1]

It is important to note, however, that in his dissent Douglas was not
advocating for the consideration of race in law school admissions,
which he did not view as the solution. Instead, he believed that contemporary testing requirements were the problem that needed to be
addressed.

As an early affirmative action test case, *DeFunis* was merely
a blip on the nation's radar screen. But four years later, *Regents of
the University of California v. Bakke* propelled its plaintiff—and,
more broadly, the divisive debate over affirmative action—to the
front pages and covers of the nation's newspapers and magazines,
onto nightly television news broadcasts, and into the American
consciousness.

Allan Bakke, a white man, applied to and was rejected by the University of California Medical School at Davis on two separate occasions. Under the University's affirmative action program, UC Davis reserved sixteen of its one hundred eligible medical school seats every year for qualified minorities, defined by the university as students who self-identified as "Black," "Chicano," "Asian," or "American Indian."[2] Because Bakke's strictly numeric academic record—a combination of undergraduate grade point average and test scores—exceeded that of some admitted minority students, Bakke argued that he was excluded from admission on the basis of race.

The question presented to the Supreme Court was whether the university's affirmative action program violated the Fourteenth Amendment's Equal Protection Clause or the Civil Rights Act of 1964. The decision: UC Davis's program was judged invalid because the applicants for the set number of seats reserved for racial minorities were insulated from competition with the larger applicant pool. The Supreme Court ruled that, in higher education, the formal guarantee of a fixed number of seats (i.e., a "quota") for minorities was prohibited.

The controversial case produced six separate opinions, none of which commanded a majority of the Court. Four Justices would have upheld the program on the ground that it is constitutionally permissible for the government to use race to remedy disadvantages imposed on minorities by past and present racial prejudice. Four others would have avoided the constitutional question altogether and struck down the program as a violation of Title VI, which prohibits discrimination on the basis of race, color, or national origin in any program or activity that receives federal funds or other federal financial assistance. (Among those four was Associate

Justice William Rehnquist, whose past concerning matters of race was checkered: As a law clerk to Justice Robert Jackson during the Court's 1952–1953 term, Rehnquist authored a memo titled "A Random Thought on the Segregation Cases." Written in anticipation of oral arguments in *Brown v. Board of Education*, the memo urged Jackson to reject arguments made by lawyers in *Brown* and to uphold *Plessy v. Ferguson*. Rehnquist wrote, "I think *Plessy v. Ferguson* was right and should be re-affirmed.")[3]

The plurality opinion in *Bakke* was written by Justice Powell, one of the four recent Nixon appointees to the Court. A highly successful corporate lawyer from Richmond, Virginia, Powell served as the chair of the Richmond Public School Board from 1952 to 1961, in which capacity he steered the city away from massive resistance tactics while doing as little as possible to end segregation.[4] Powell was nonetheless on the record in support of equal rights. He wrote in 1968, "We must come to grips realistically with the gravest domestic problem of this century. America has the resources, and our people have the compassion and desire, to provide equal justice, adequate education and job opportunities for all. This, surely, we must do."[5]

In *Bakke*, Powell provided a fifth vote to invalidate UC Davis's affirmative action program, but he also rejected the state court's injunction prohibiting *any* consideration of race in university admissions.

Powell's plurality opinion, joined in part by four other Justices (Brennan, White, Marshall, and Blackmun) provided the roadmap for judicial assessment of affirmative action programs for decades to come. In his opinion Powell refused to declare that universities could *never* consider an applicant's race without violating the Fourteenth Amendment's Equal Protection Clause. Rather, in his view, race could be considered as one of several factors in college admissions policy—but not the deciding factor. Affirmative action programs were justified, Powell asserted, only for the purpose of pursuing the vague objective of "educational diversity." Accordingly, his opinion de-emphasized justice for Black students in favor of focusing on "enriching" the higher educational experience for all.

The state had a compelling interest, Powell believed, in promoting diversity in the interest of pluralism, especially in the realm of education. He came to this conclusion after traveling in 1958 with a delegation from the American Bar Association to the Soviet Union, where he observed up close the effects of an ideologically undiversified education system. In a report of the trip titled "Soviet Education: Means Towards World Domination," Powell noted that "the entire educational system" in the Soviet Union "is planned and operated with the purpose of thoroughly indoctrinating every child with Marxism; the theme that the Marxist always triumphs is an ever present one, and the inevitability and 'justness' of the 'class struggle' is taught both directly and indirectly."[6] This was not education, Powell concluded. This was indoctrination. Viewpoint diversity was a vital part of education insofar as it contributed to the capacity of students to come to their own conclusions about the world.

Powell's opinion in *Bakke* was informed, in part, by his contention that deploying race-based classification in the admissions policies would not sit well with the white majority of the U.S. population. "All state-imposed classifications that rearrange burdens and benefits on the basis of race," Powell wrote, "are likely to be viewed with deep resentment by the individuals burdened."[7] The "burdened individuals" to which Powell was referring: white students not granted admission.

He elaborated further:

Race or ethnic background may be deemed a "plus" in a particular applicant's file. . . yet it does not insulate the individual from comparison with all other candidates for the available seats. The file of a particular black applicant may be examined for his potential contribution to diversity without the factor of race being decisive when compared, for example, with that of an applicant identified as an Italian-American if the latter is thought to exhibit qualities more likely to promote beneficial educational pluralism. Such qualities could include exceptional personal talents, unique work or service experience, leadership potential, maturity, demonstrated compassion, a history of overcoming disadvantage, ability to communicate with the poor, or other qualifications deemed important. In short, an admissions program operated in this way is flexible enough to consider all pertinent elements of diversity in light of the particular qualifications of each applicant, and to place them on the same footing for consideration, although not necessarily according them the same weight. Indeed, the weight attributed to a particular quality may vary from year to year depending upon the "mix" both of the student body and the applicants for the incoming class.[8]

Powell sought, on one hand, to protect opportunity for minority students; on the other, he sought simultaneously to appease white students. But what he may have perceived to be a pragmatic, middle-ground opinion within a divided Court dramatically reframed the affirmative action issue. For, instead of defending affirmative action as a way to promote equality and inclusion, the decision was informed by Powell's interest in giving colleges and universities the right to cultivate diversity among the student body as an educational attribute.

Justice Brennan, joined by Justices White, Marshall, and Blackmun, wrote separately, acknowledging the paradigm at the center of affirmative action by opening with the statement, "Our Nation was founded on the principle that 'all Men are created equal.' Yet candor requires acknowledgment that the Framers of our Constitution, to forge the 13 Colonies into one Nation, openly compromised this principle of equality with its antithesis: slavery."[9] Further, Brennan noted, *Bakke* was being decided less than twenty-five years after *Brown*, and that inequality had not been eradicated with "all deliberate speed," as *Brown II* had demanded. He added, "Claims that law must be 'colorblind' or that the datum of race is no longer relevant to public policy must be seen as aspiration, rather than as description of reality. This is not to denigrate aspiration; for reality rebukes us that race has too often been used by those who would stigmatize and oppress minorities. Yet we cannot—and, as we shall demonstrate, need not under our Constitution or Title VI, which merely extends the constraints of the Fourteenth Amendment to private parties who receive federal funds—let color blindness become myopia which masks the reality that many 'created equal' have been treated within our lifetimes as inferior both by the law and by their fellow citizens."[10]

Justice Marshall also wrote a separate opinion, which was more focused on the Black experience in American history. He challenged Powell's view that remedying past discrimination could not justify a university's affirmative action program, asserting that there was "ample support for the conclusion that a university can employ race-conscious measures to remedy past societal discrimination, without the need for a finding that those benefited were actually victims of that discrimination," in light of the nation's long history of discrimination against its Black citizens. "I do not agree that petitioner's admissions program violates the Constitution," he wrote. "For it must be remembered that, during most of the past 200 years, the Constitution, as interpreted by this Court, did not prohibit the most ingenious and pervasive forms of discrimination against the Negro. Now, when a State acts to remedy the effects of that legacy of discrimination, I cannot believe that this same Constitution stands as a barrier."[11]

Marshall highlighted the failed legacy of constitutional law as both arbiter and enforcer in the racial arena. Not only did the courts uphold segregation, but even when the Court struck down certain laws that denied Black citizens "the opportunity to become doctors, lawyers, engineers, and the like," the decisions "did not automatically end segregation, nor did they move Negroes from a position of legal inferiority to equality. The legacy of years of slavery and of years of second-class citizenship in the wake of emancipation could not be so easily eliminated."[12]

His opinion is a devastating indictment of white America's oppression of Black Americans. It juxtaposes the two hundred years of slavery, 1787's Three-fifths Compromise (which, for the purpose of apportioning the seats in the U.S. House of Representatives, counted enslaved Black persons as three-fifths of a person), and Jim Crow, all of which were defined by a systemic mission to deprive Black Americans of their freedoms. And in that asymmetry—and the contention among some observers that the Constitution was, or is, "race blind"—Marshall noted that it is "more than a little ironic that, after several hundred years of class-based discrimination against Negroes, the Court is unwilling to hold that a class-based remedy for that discrimination is permissible."[13]

Marshall agreed with Powell that there was a compelling state interest in diversifying higher education, but that interest was dwarfed by the broader necessity of securing justice and equality for Black Americans. "In light of the sorry history of discrimination and its devastating impact on the lives of Negroes," Marshall concluded, "bringing the Negro into the mainstream of American life should be a state interest of the highest order. To fail to do so is to ensure that America will forever remain a divided society."[14] Marshall's former colleagues at the NAACP concurred, viewing *Bakke* as a defeat for civil rights.[15] In the end, the contours of private attitudes, public discourse, and the Court's affirmative action decision making for the next four decades reflected Justice Powell's vision and not Justice Marshall's.

Bakke, then, fundamentally inverted affirmative action's intent. Before this decision, the implicit promise and focus of affirmative action was to improve opportunity for Black students; after *Bakke*, the focus shifted to ensuring that all students (the majority of them white), by studying in a diverse environment, would accrue "the general benefits of diversity."

The ruling radically changed the college admission officer's role. Before *Bakke*, he or she was focused on trying to help improve the lot of Black students—to create real and meaningful opportunities for intellectual, social, and economic advancement to a defined cohort of students whose parents, grandparents, and beyond had been unable to and in fact legally prohibited from competing on a level academic playing field with white people. After *Bakke*, the admissions officer's role was akin to that of a social planner or dinner party host tasked with assembling a diverse roster of guests who, once convened, would as a result of their differing experiences and conversational exchanges mutually increase their collective knowledge.

BEYOND *BAKKE*

Justice Powell's opinion anticipated a backlash against affirmative action that gained momentum during the 1980s. Large swaths of the nation, fatigued after more than twenty years of turmoil related to civil rights- and Vietnam, longed for a fresh start, for a return to "simpler times," for what the Reagan administration would eventually describe as "Morning in America." For many, notably white, Americans, there was an impulse to declare that the playing field had indeed been leveled for Black Americans and that the unpleasant legacy of racial discrimination could, finally, be put to rest.

Despite Powell's hope that his opinion would arrest inklings of "deep resentment" among white people, the sentiment was instead deliberately aroused by affirmative action's foes. The concept of "reverse discrimination" raised in *Bakke* was seized on by 1980 presidential candidate Ronald Reagan, who promised to dismantle "federal guidelines or quotas which require race, ethnicity, or sex . . . to be the principal factor in hiring or education." During his years as governor of California, Reagan had been a staunch opponent of busing and affirmative action.[16] As president, he was an open advocate for what he called a "color-blind" society, a term that enveloped his opposition to quotas or mandatory minority hiring goals.[17] His promises were transformed into policy after he was elected president: The Reagan administration refused to enforce many civil rights laws, replaced pro–affirmative action appointees, and dismantled affirmative action hiring programs established under Richard Nixon.[18]

A related trend that accelerated in the 1980s was for members of the entrenched white establishment to recast affirmative action's traditional promise and obligation to deliver justice and opportunity to historically disenfranchised groups into a form of *noblesse oblige*, as Reagan's interior secretary, James Watt, infamously, and condescendingly, did in September 1983. In a speech before the U.S. Chamber of Commerce, Watt "jokingly" described an expert panel he convened: "I have a black, a woman, two Jews and a cripple. And we have talent," Watt declared.[19] The comment sparked outrage, and less than three weeks later, Watt announced his resignation. Tellingly, in a written statement, Reagan "reluctantly" accepted Watt's resignation—without commenting on or denouncing the disgraced cabinet secretary's comments.[20]

By the decade's end, Ronald Regan had appointed Justices Sandra Day O'Connor, Antonin Scalia, and Anthony Kennedy to the Supreme Court, followed, in 1991, by Clarence Thomas, appointed by George H. W. Bush. In the coming years, Justices Thomas and Scalia would side with the conservative wing of the Court on affirmative action issues, whereas Justices Kennedy and O'Connor adopted more middle-of-the road positions. Affirmative action was under threat.

Hostility to the policy was explicitly expressed in the 1990 Senate race in North Carolina, where conservative firebrand Jesse Helms, running for his fourth term, was in the political fight of his life. His opponent was Harvey Gantt, an architect and Democratic politician from Charlotte, where he had served as the city's first Black mayor from 1983 to 1987. Behind in the polls, the Helms campaign began airing a set of overtly racist campaign advertisements. In one ad, a pair of white hands holds an employment rejection letter. The hands then tear up the letter as the narrator says: "You needed that job. And you were the best qualified. But they had to give it to a minority because of a racial quota. Is that really fair?"[21] The ad helped

Helms secure victory in a tight race by a narrow margin, squeaking by with only 53 percent of the vote.[22]

The "rejection letter" campaign ad resonated, especially among working-class white Americans, who, by the early 1990s, were growing increasingly anxious as their economic fortunes and concomitant social status began not only to stagnate but slip. The years between the end of World War II and 1970 marked a period of economic prosperity and upward social mobility unrivaled in human history and accompanied by American economic dominance around the globe. Americans of all races and social classes shared in the nation's largesse: Real income grew by 2.25 percent per year. Designated "The Golden Age of American capitalism" by economists, in this period millions of Americans ascended to the middle class, became first-time homeowners, sent the first children in their lineage to college or university, and enjoyed the trappings of consumer society: labor-saving household appliances, new automobiles, and vacations.[23] Not only did everyone's economic fortunes improve during those years, the gap between rich and poor also narrowed in what economists would later dub the "Great Compression."

By the 1970s, though, the growth began to slow. And 1981, a year in which the country was gripped by recession, definitively marked the end of the postwar boom. Aside from wage stagnation, which has afflicted the working class ever since, the income inequality gap began to widen. As the economy evolved from an industrial to a service- and information-driven economy, the top earners increasingly captured a larger share of the pie. According to the Economic Policy Institute, between approximately 1980 and 2020 the hourly pay of a typical American worker increased 17.5 percent;[24] in the same four decades, CEO pay skyrocketed 1,322 percent.[25] In the early 1990s the top 5 percent of earners took home about 20 percent of total income; two decades later, the top 1 percent captured more than 20 percent of total income. Accordingly, by the time Jesse Helms aired his odious campaign advertisement, Americans who for decades may have prided themselves on their capacity for generosity—and supported "redistributive" federal initiatives like Social Security, Medicare, Aid to Families with Dependent Children, and even affirmative action—now confronted shrinking paychecks, higher taxes, and fierce competition for jobs, eroding their support for such policies.[26]

Columbia Law School professor Kimberlé Crenshaw, who has for more than three decades been one of the nation's leading scholars on race and gender issues, has argued that the embedded nature of white economic, political, and cultural dominance in American society caused white people to "question the legitimacy of racial remedies that relied upon a suspension of these myths" of equal opportunity. Crenshaw wrote: "Whites were on the defensive, not because the promise of vestedness had proven unstable, but because Black people had been granted some privileges at their expense." Retrenchment in antidiscrimination law, then, was the result of white backlash "against Blacks and against institutions perceived as sympathetic to Black interests."[27]

The year 1996 was particularly noteworthy in the evolution— or, rather, devolution—of affirmative action. That year, California voters approved, with 55 percent of the vote, Proposition 209.[28] The state's constitution was duly amended: "The California Constitution prohibits the state, including any political subdivision or government instrumentality of or within the state, from . . . granting preferential treatment to, any individual or group on the basis of race, sex, color, ethnicity, or national origin in the operation of public employment, public education, or public contracting."[29] The measure followed the University of California system's action, a year earlier, of passing two measures, SP-1 and SP-2, that contained similar provisions.[30]

A quarter century after the passage of Proposition 209, there has been a remarkable lack of progress in diversity in the California university system, as several empirical studies have indicated.[31] At the University of California at Berkeley, for example, Black students account for a mere 3 percent of the freshman class—down from between 6 percent and 7 percent before enactment of Proposition 209.[32]

During the 1980s and 1990s, while civil rights advocates, elected officials, the news media, and the public were primarily focused on the racial dimension of the affirmative action debate, lurking beneath the surface, and less discussed, was the economic dimension of the story. Excluded from California's premier institutions of higher learning, Black students and other underrepresented minorities cascaded into lower-quality public and private universities. According to research conducted at the University of California at Berkeley's Goldman School of Public Policy, which tracked minority students who attended California colleges and universities between 1994 and 2002, Proposition 209 had caused a cumulative decline in Black students' earning power, translating, by the mid-2010s, into a 5 percent annual wage decline for Black students between ages twenty-four and thirty-four.[33]

Despite evidence that minority graduates' wages suffered as a result of the state's policy against affirmative action, in 2020, when a new ballot initiative, Proposition 16, sought to repeal Proposition 209, the measure was rejected by California voters by a margin of 57 percent to 43 percent, suggesting that their hostility toward affirmative action had actually *increased.* This despite the fact that in the years between Proposition 209 and Proposition 16, academic research affirmed what common sense already suggested: Attending a top college increases earnings for minority students. Two studies by Alan Krueger of Princeton University and Stacy Dale of Mathematica Policy Research, the first published in 2002[34] and the second, a follow up study published in 2011,[35] examined the relation between earnings potential and the college students attended in 1976 and 1989, respectively. For African American and Hispanic students in the 1976 group, attendance at a selective school provided 6.7 percent higher earnings for the period of 2003–2007; the 1989 group saw a 12 percent rate of return on attending a selective school.

The litigation continued, too. In 1996 the Supreme Court declined to grant certiorari to hear *Hopwood v. Texas*, thereby refusing to disrupt a Fifth Circuit decision striking down a university's affirmative action admission policy.

In *Hopwood*, the University of Texas at Austin's School of Law was sued over its race-conscious admissions policy. After being rejected by the law school in 1992, Cheryl Hopwood, a white woman, filed a federal lawsuit arguing that the university discriminated against her on the basis of race. United States District Judge Sam Sparks, a graduate of the University of Texas School of Law, presided over the case. He ruled that the university could continue to use racial preferences in its admissions process—not a rigid quota of minority seats for admission, but a flexible process by which race was taken into account in order to achieve diversity in the student body— noting that while it was "regrettable that affirmative action programs are still needed in our society," they were still "a necessity" until society could overcome its legacy of institutional racism.[36]

Hopwood appealed to the Fifth Circuit Court of Appeals, which held, despite Justice Powell's opinion in *Bakke*, that diversity was *not* a compelling justification for the use of racial classifications in applications. The opinion read, in part, "Within the general principles of the Fourteenth Amendment, the use of race in admissions for diversity in higher education contradicts, rather than furthers, the aims of equal protection. Diversity fosters, rather than minimizes, the use of race. It treats minorities as a group, rather than as individuals."[37] Accordingly, the court held that "the University of Texas School of Law may not use race as a factor in deciding which applicants to admit in order to achieve a diverse student body, to combat the perceived effects of a hostile environment at the law school, to alleviate the law school's poor reputation in the minority community, or to eliminate any present effects of past discrimination by actors other than the law school."[38]

This time, the university sought review. By the time the case made its way to the Supreme Court, the university had already abandoned the challenged admissions procedure, but it urged the Court to nonetheless grant review to consider whether the Fifth Circuit's reasoning was sound. The Supreme Court declined to hear the case.[39]

Thus the decision stood as controlling law in the Fifth Circuit. Consequently, universities in the states of Texas, Louisiana, and Mississippi were prohibited from using racial preferences for the next seven years, until *Hopwood* was abrogated by a landmark case that would set the tone for the ongoing debate over affirmative action for the next two decades: *Grutter v. Bollinger* (2003), in which one of the co-authors of this book was a named defendant (along with the University of Michigan and several other individuals) and led the litigation as president of the university.

GRUTTER V. BOLLINGER (2003) AND GRATZ V. BOLLINGER (2003)

The facts of the *Grutter* case were similar to the challenges to affirmative action that preceded it: Barbara Grutter applied to the

University of Michigan Law School with a 3.81 grade point average and a 161 on the LSAT, numbers that ranked in the 86th percentile among applicants. Grutter was rejected and agreed to become the named plaintiff in a suit brought against the university by the Center for Individual Rights, which opposed the law school's race-conscious admission policies.[40] (The Center for Individual Rights, a libertarian public-interest law firm founded in the late 1980s, funded the plaintiffs' litigation in *Hopwood*, in *Grutter*, and in another University of Michigan admissions case that would be combined with the *Grutter* case before the Supreme Court, *Gratz v. Bollinger*.)[41]

At the dawn of the new century, those of us who supported affirmative action in higher education knew that the headwinds we had experienced since the 1980s—socially, politically, and in the courts—remained formidable. Accordingly, we recognized that if we continued to fight the old fight, in the old ways, we would change neither hearts, nor minds, nor the law. So in response to what was now perceived to be an existential threat to higher education's mission, we amended both strategies and tactics: We indicated that we would fight to the finish (no settlement); we would link the policy of affirmative action to *Brown* (not *Bakke*); we would enlist support from all universities (e.g., the American Association of Universities, representing America's leading research universities) and many sectors of society (e.g., major corporations and the U.S. military on behalf of their academies) in order to show broad support for the policy as well as to communicate that if affirmative action in higher education were suspended, all the cumulative efforts of the previous four decades to address racism in the society would start to unravel; and, finally, we would defend the affirmative action position publicly and not follow the usual practice of being silent during litigation.

In March 2001 U.S. District Court Judge Bernard Friedman ruled in the plaintiff's favor.[42] The University of Michigan appealed the decision. In May 2002 the Sixth Circuit Court of Appeals reversed the district court's decision. Citing *Bakke*, the appellate court held that the law school could properly use race as one of several factors in its admissions program to further the "compelling interest" of diversity.

When the plaintiffs petitioned for Supreme Court review, the Michigan legal team had a decision to make. The university had won on appeal. Under such circumstances, most defendants would be inclined to leave well enough alone and vigorously oppose an attempt to have the case heard by the Supreme Court. There was good reason to do so: Michigan had won by only a narrow margin; in the Sixth Circuit, Michigan did not receive the conservative judges' votes. Further, the university's legal team harbored no illusions that the Supreme Court's conservative jurists—Chief Justice William Rehnquist and Associate Justices Antonin Scalia, Sandra Day O'Connor, the libertarian-leaning Anthony Kennedy, and most notably Clarence Thomas, himself a beneficiary of affirmative action as a student at Yale Law but nonetheless a harsh critic of the policy—would uphold the Sixth Circuit's ruling. Besides, affirmative action programs in higher education remained protected in the vast majority of states. The programs may have been flawed in most college presidents' and admissions officers' view, but at least they remained legal. Sometimes, as many affirmative action proponents argued, protecting a less-than-perfect status quo is preferable to the possibility that a half-century-old program could be nullified by the Court.

Alternatively, many supporters of affirmative action believed the time was right to challenge the Court—and society—to reconsider the vague and, frankly, unhelpful precedent established by *Bakke*. As a result, a strategy was adopted that contained equal measures of caution and audacity. The Michigan legal team opposed certiorari—that is, Supreme Court review of the appeals court's decision—but suggested that *if* the Court took on *Grutter*, it should also include another Michigan-related admissions case, *Gratz v. Bollinger*. Because the law school and the undergraduate programs had adopted differing affirmative action policies, presenting the two cases simultaneously would allow Michigan to test both programs' legality before the Court.

The facts of the *Gratz* case: In 1995 Jennifer Gratz was denied admission to the University of Michigan's College of Literature, Science, and the Arts, under an admissions policy that differed from the law school's in the way race was considered. In the undergraduate program the university used a 150-point scale to rank applicants, with 100 points needed to guarantee admission. The undergraduate program gave underrepresented ethnic groups, including African Americans, Hispanics, and Native Americans, an automatic 20-point bonus toward their score.[43] By contrast, the law school's admissions program did not award specific points to minority applicants but, rather, considered race as one factor and sought to achieve a "critical mass" of minority students in each class.

The Supreme Court agreed to combine and hear both cases— the first time the Court would hear a case on affirmative action in education since the *Bakke* decision twenty-five years earlier.

As a matter of legal strategy, the Michigan defense team was determined to underscore the notion that grades and test scores, while key factors in admission, were not and should not be the *only* deciding factor. A candidate's background, life experience, moxie, and potential to represent the university well after -graduation were also important factors in an admissions officer's decision. Further, the defense team was determined to show that Black and other minority candidates were not competing on a level playing field in the admissions game.

Finally, the proponents of affirmative action enlisted vocal allies from across society. To that end, ninety amicus briefs were filed by selective colleges and universities, the military, large publicly traded companies, and other organizations that supported race-conscious programs.[44]

On April 1, 2003, the Supreme Court heard oral arguments in *Grutter* and *Gratz*. The Court allowed the recordings of the arguments to be released to the public the same day—only the second time it had done so. (The first time was in *Bush v. Gore*, in 2000, which ultimately ended the 2000 presidential election.)

In *Grutter*, the university defended its admissions practices, explaining that it had a compelling interest in fostering a diverse student body. However, the university also acknowledged the need for limits on race-conscious programs; the legal team knew better than to argue for a rigid quota system, and it sought to distinguish the law school's admissions process from such a system. Accordingly, the university explained that minority law school admissions between 1993 and 2000 had ranged from 42 to 73, so there was no evidence to suggest that a fixed number of seats were reserved for minority candidates.[45]

During oral arguments, Justice Scalia, while questioning Maureen Mahoney, Michigan's attorney, challenged the notion that the university had a "compelling interest" in diversifying its student body. Further, he asserted, Michigan had created its own problem by being a selective law school, knowing that would erect barriers to entry for minorities:

> "I find it hard to take seriously the State of Michigan's contention that racial diversity is a compelling State interest, compelling

enough to warrant ignoring the Constitution's prohibition of discrimination on the basis of race," Justice Scalia said to Ms. Mahoney. "The reason I say that is that the problem is a problem of Michigan's own creation, that is to say, it has decided to create an elite law school, it is one of the best law schools in the country. And there are few State law schools that—that get to that level. Now, it's done this by taking only the best students with the best grades and the best SATs or LSATs . . . knowing that the result of this will be to exclude to a large degree minorities. . . . Nonetheless, Michigan says we want an elite law school. Now, having created this situation by making that decision, it then turns around and says, oh, we have a compelling State interest in eliminating this racial imbalance that we ourselves have created. Now, if Michigan really cares enough about that racial imbalance, why doesn't it do as many other State law schools do, lower the standards, not have a flagship elite law school, it solves the problem."[46]

To this Mahoney replied, "Your Honor, I don't think there's anything in this Court's cases that suggests that the law school has to make an election between academic excellence and racial diversity."[47] As a matter of policy, Michigan asserted, it could, and did, routinely choose both.

The Court's decision was issued quickly—just eleven weeks after argument. Justice O'Connor wrote the majority opinion in *Grutter*, which held that the law school's admission policy was constitutional, because it was narrowly tailored to serve the compelling interest of attaining a diverse student body. *Grutter* was the first case in which a majority of the Court adopted a majority position holding affirmative action constitutional under the Fourteenth Amendment (albeit one following from Justice

Powell's solo opinion in *Bakke* focusing on attaining a diverse student body).

On the other hand, in *Gratz*, the majority held that the admission policy violated the Equal Protection Clause, because although diversity is a compelling objective, the weight attached to the race factor in the undergraduate admissions process was simply too great. The Court determined that the policy did not provide individual consideration of applicants but, rather, relied on the admission of nearly every applicant of "underrepresented minority" status. Chief Justice Rehnquist's majority opinion explained that the university "automatically distributes 20 points to every single applicant from an 'underrepresented minority' group, as defined by the University. The only consideration that accompanies this distribution of points is a factual review of an application to determine whether an individual is a member of one of these minority groups. Moreover, unlike Justice Powell's example [in *Bakke*], where the race of a 'particular black applicant' could be considered without being decisive, the [university's] automatic distribution of 20 points has the effect of making the 'factor of race . . . decisive' for virtually every minimally qualified underrepresented minority applicant."[48] In short, the Court left the door open for Michigan and other universities to continue using racial preferences to promote diversity as one, but not the sole, determinant of admission.

In *Grutter*, Justice O'Connor wrote that in order for schools to ensure that they enrolled a "critical mass" of minority students, in part so that these students "do not feel isolated or like spokespersons for their race,"[49] schools could continue to consider race as a factor in individual admissions. This would promote diversity and prepare all students for a diverse marketplace in the future. One novel justification offered by O'Connor was a national need for diverse leadership, which could only happen with an adequately diverse educational system. "Moreover, universities, and in particular, law schools, represent the training ground for a large number of our Nation's leaders. . . . In order to cultivate a set of leaders with legitimacy in the eyes of the citizenry, it is necessary that the path to leadership be visibly open to talented and qualified individuals of every race and ethnicity. All members of our heterogeneous society must have confidence in the openness and integrity of the educational institutions that provide this training."[50]

While the decision in *Grutter* was 5–4, six Justices considered diversity a compelling governmental interest, and only two (Thomas and Scalia) specifically disagreed. Surprisingly Chief Justice Rehnquist voiced no view on whether diversity could ever be a compelling governmental interest.

It is worth noting that *Grutter* was not a typical equal protection case. It was not bound in the intricacies of prevailing equal protection law. Instead of analyzing whether the traditional requirements of strict scrutiny—a compelling government interest met through narrowly tailored means—were satisfied, O'Connor wrote that "[t]he Law School's educational judgment that such diversity is essential to its education mission is one to which we defer."[51]

One of the key outcomes of *Grutter*, especially when read together with *Gratz*, was that quota systems were likely to be found unconstitutional. Similarly, individualized reviews that considered race could no longer employ a fixed point system (like that seen in *Gratz*), which would likely result in race being weighed too heavily in the candidate selection process to pass constitutional muster. Between the two opinions, *Grutter* is the more important, because it established the basic ground rules under which institutions of higher education could employ affirmative action policies moving forward.

O'Connor, in the closing of the opinion, surprisingly assigned to racism an expiration date, a time when America, ostensibly, would be truly colorblind. The year she selected as the "logical end point" for affirmative action programs: 2028.[52] As she wrote in 2003: "We expect that 25 years from now, the use of racial preferences will no longer be necessary to further the interest approved now."[53] Given the conditions under which minorities—especially Black Americans—were living in 2003 and continue to live today, the prediction she issued registers not as prescient but as tragically naïve. And, from a legal perspective, strikingly odd: We cannot emphasize how unusual it is for a constitutional principle to contain an arbitrarily assigned "sunset clause." Ironically, the most historically noteworthy antecedent to O'Connor's sunset clause is the one included in Article 1, Section 9, Clause 1 of the United States Constitution of 1789, "The Slave Trade Clause," which prohibited a ban on the importation of enslaved persons until 1808.[54]

Justices Ginsburg and Breyer concurred in *Grutter* but wrote separately to express skepticism about the sunset provision. In their separate opinion they emphasized that "conscious and unconscious race bias, even rank discrimination based on race, remain alive in our land."[55] Further, they added, "From today's vantage point, one may hope, but not firmly forecast, that over the next generation's span, progress toward nondiscrimination and genuinely equal opportunity will make it safe to sunset affirmative action."[56]

Grutter prompted five separate opinions in addition to Justice O'Connor's majority opinion: concurrence in part and dissent in part from Justice Thomas (joined by Justice Scalia) and the dissent from Chief Justice Rehnquist (joined by Justices Thomas, Scalia, and Kennedy).

Justice Thomas opened by quoting Frederick Douglass: "In regard to the colored people, there is always more that is benevolent,

I perceive, than just, manifested towards us. What I ask for the negro is not benevolence, not pity, not sympathy, but simply *justice*. The American people have always been anxious to know what they shall do with us. . . . I have had but one answer from the beginning. Do nothing with us!"[57]

Thomas went on to condemn the majority for approving Michigan's admissions policy, saying that the Court validated the "Law School's racial discrimination not by interpreting the people's Constitution, but by responding to a faddish slogan of the cognoscenti."[58] He also criticized Justice O'Connor's opinion for failing to actually apply strict scrutiny, arguing that the meaning of the Constitution does not change with time and that the Equal Protection Clause should not mean something different in twenty-five years. "The Constitution abhors classifications based on race," he wrote, "not only because those classifications can harm favored races or are based on illegitimate motives, but also because every time the government places citizens on racial registers and makes race relevant to the provision of burdens or benefits, it demeans us all."[59]

Thomas also contrasted the University of Michigan's admissions policies with UC Berkeley's, maintaining that the latter was able to maintain minority enrollment despite Proposition 209's ban on considering race in admissions. Since Proposition 209 had become law, he noted, "total underrepresented minority student enrollment at Boalt Hall [UC Berkeley's law school] now exceeds 1996 levels. Apparently the Michigan Law School cannot be counted on to be as resourceful. The Court is willfully blind to the very real experience in California and elsewhere, which raises the inference that institutions with 'reputation[s] for excellence' . . . rivaling the [Michigan] Law School's have satisfied their sense of mission without resorting to prohibited racial discrimination."[60]

Chief Justice Rehnquist's dissent criticized the University of Michigan Law School's program as too vague, too unwieldy, and too amorphous to be a governing standard in a dynamic admissions office. "The Law School's disparate admissions practices with respect to these minority groups demonstrate that its alleged goal of 'critical mass' is simply a sham," the Chief Justice wrote.[61]

While the outcomes of *Grutter* and *Gratz* resulted in a legal standard that protected affirmative action, the standard was only a qualified victory for affirmative action's proponents. The courts—and many in American society—continued to confuse "not discriminating" against Black citizens with "creating opportunity" for Black citizens to integrate into, and ascend within, the ranks of American society. At the most basic level, then, *Grutter* represented a victory for defenders of the affirmative action status quo, as opposed to an embrace of the pre-*Bakke* conception of affirmative action for which the defendants had hoped.

THE ROBERTS COURT

In 2005 Chief Justice Rehnquist died and twenty-six days later, John Roberts—a foe of affirmative action policy dating back to his time as an attorney in the Reagan administration[62]—took the Constitutional and Judicial Oaths at the White House to become the Seventeenth Chief Justice of the United States.[63] A little more than a year later, the next divisive affirmative action case would ascend to the high court: 2007's *Parents Involved in Community Schools v. Seattle School District No. 1 (PICS)*.

At issue were efforts for voluntary school desegregation and integration in Seattle, Washington, and Louisville, Kentucky. Both school districts voluntarily used individualized racial classifications to achieve diversity and to avoid racial isolation through student assignment.

The Seattle School District allowed students to apply to any high school in its district. Predictably, some schools were more popular among students and their families than others, and they became oversubscribed. In order to rebalance student distribution districtwide, school administrators initiated a "tiebreaker" scheme to decide which students would be admitted to the most popular schools. Race was one of the factors used to determine a tiebreaker because it advanced the district's goal of maintaining diversity. If the racial demographics of any school's student body deviated by more than a predetermined number of percentage points from those of Seattle's total student population (approximately 40 percent white and 60 percent non-white), the racial tiebreaker went into effect. A nonprofit group, Parents Involved in Community Schools, sued, arguing that the racial tiebreaker violated the Equal Protection Clause of the Fourteenth Amendment, the Civil Rights Act of 1964, and Washington state law.

A federal district court dismissed the suit, upholding the tiebreaker system, and the Ninth Circuit affirmed.

In the Kentucky case that was eventually consolidated with *PICS*, Jefferson County adopted a plan requiring all nonmagnet schools to maintain a minimum Black enrollment of 15 percent and a maximum Black enrollment of 50 percent. There too, the district court found that the school district had asserted a compelling interest in maintaining racially diverse schools and that its plan was narrowly tailored to serve that interest. The Sixth Circuit affirmed.

The Supreme Court granted review and consolidated the cases, which were argued in early December 2006. Seven months later, the Court issued its decision. It split 4–1–4 on various elements of the case, with Justice Kennedy writing the swing vote opinion. He concurred with Chief Justice Roberts and Justices Scalia, Thomas, and Alito that the programs used by Jefferson County and Seattle were unconstitutional, contending that the districts failed to demonstrate that their processes were sufficiently tailored to pass strict scrutiny. But Kennedy also agreed with the dissent—authored by Justice Breyer and joined by Justices Stevens, Souter, and Ginsburg—that schools *can* attempt to avoid racial isolation and promote diversity by considering the racial makeup of schools.[64] In Kennedy's view, however, it would be preferable to "devise race-conscious measures to address the problem in a general way and without treating each student in a different fashion solely on the basis of a systematic, individual typing by race."[65]

Roberts's plurality opinion contended that K-12 cases were not governed by *Grutter*, noting that "considerations unique to institutions of higher education" were not applicable to K-12 schools. According to Roberts, "universities occupy a special niche in our constitutional tradition" because of "the expansive freedoms of speech and thought associated with the university environment."[66] Even setting aside the propriety of a diversity rationale in this context, in Roberts's view, this case was more similar to *Gratz* than to *Grutter*: The means used by the school district weighed race so heavily that it was akin to the quota or allocation system of the kind the Court had rejected as insufficiently individualized in *Gratz*.[67]

The plurality opinion also emphasized that the Court's past cases had recognized that the Constitution permitted government consideration of race only for two compelling purposes: remedying "the effects of past intentional discrimination" and promoting diversity in education as "part of a broader assessment of diversity, and not simply an effort to achieve racial balance."[68] The plurality rejected nonremedial considerations, highlighting that government consideration of race to promote integration was offensive "racial balancing," and concluded by invoking the colorblindness reading of *Brown*: "For schools that never segregated on the basis of race, such as Seattle, or that have removed the vestiges of past segregation, such as Jefferson County [KY], the way 'to achieve a system of determining admission to the public schools on a nonracial basis' is to stop assigning students on a racial basis."[69]

Yale Law School professor Reva Siegel observed: "Justice Kennedy agrees with Chief Justice Roberts's plurality opinion that government policies employing racial classifications for benign purposes are subject to strict scrutiny and that the schools' use of racial classifications in the instant case is not narrowly tailored. But he then proceeds to emphasize his differences with the Chief Justice. . . . Justice Kennedy insists that colorblindness cannot be construed as a rule that inhibits government from acting to promote its legitimate interest in the racial integration of schools."[70]

That notion harkened back to *Brown*, reviving a debate between proponents of equality in the letter of the law and proponents of equitable remedies for past discrimination—and which should guide the constitutional debate.

In an emotional twenty-minute speech from the bench, Justice Stephen Breyer, in the principal dissenting opinion, denounced the majority opinion as "radical": "It is not often in the law that so few have so quickly changed so much," Breyer said of the Court's decision.[71] Similarly, Justice John Paul Stevens wrote a sharply worded dissent in which he accused the plurality of abandoning the promises of *Brown*: "The Court has changed significantly since it decided *School Comm. of Boston* in 1968 [in which the Supreme Court upheld a Massachusetts Supreme Judicial Court decision upholding the constitutionality of that city's public school desegregation program]. It was then more faithful to *Brown* and more respectful of our precedent than it is today. It is my firm conviction that no Member of the Court that I joined in 1975 would have agreed with today's decision."[72]

The debate raged on, in the court of public opinion and in the Supreme Court. In *Fisher v. University of Texas* (*"Fisher I,"* 2013), the Court vacated a Fifth Circuit decision upholding the challenged program on the grounds that the court's narrow tailoring analysis improperly deferred to the university's judgment regarding the method of achieving diversity. Following remand, the Court heard the case a second time in *Fisher II*, this time affirming the Fifth Circuit's decision that the process used by the University of Texas at Austin did not violate the Equal Protection Clause. Both of these cases underscored the Court's desire to consider racial diversity only in terms of its overall educational benefit, without acknowledging the persistent reality of race in America.

A brief history of *Fisher*: In 1997 the Texas legislature enacted a law requiring the University of Texas to admit all high school seniors who ranked in the top 10 percent of their high school class. Ironically, this new method of achieving a racially and ethnically diverse student body would be effective (partly, it turned out) because the public school K-12 system was itself highly segregated. Following the *Hopwood* decision, the University of Texas had adopted a race-neutral admissions policy. Now the university complied with the legislature's new mandate. For the remainder of the in-state freshman class, though, the university determined it needed to consider race as a factor in admissions in order to achieve its diversity goals. In 2008 Abigail Fisher, a white woman from Fort Bend County, Texas, applied to the university and was denied admission.[73] Fisher, who was not in the top 10 percent of her class and thus was not guaranteed a seat, was as a result compelled to compete for one of the 841 slots reserved for lower--tier students.[74] Thus she joined a pool from which a fixed number of applicants could still gain admission by scoring high on non-academic metrics: personal talents, leadership qualities, family circumstances, and so on. One such non-academic metric was race. Fisher alleged that the university had discriminated against her and her co-plaintiffs on the basis of their race, in violation of the Equal Protection Clause of the Fourteenth Amendment.[75]

The district court upheld the university's policy, finding that it met the standards laid out in *Grutter*, and the Fifth Circuit affirmed.[76] The Supreme Court put the case on the calendar for the term beginning in October 2012, prompting concerns among many that if the Court overruled *Grutter*, affirmative action at public universities in the United States would, in effect, end.

In *Fisher I*, however, the Court did not pass judgment on the broader issue of whether affirmative action was constitutional, but instead held only that the Fifth Circuit did not apply strict scrutiny correctly in its decision affirming the admissions policy. The Fifth Circuit erred, the Court held, by deferring to the university's conclusion that its admissions program was narrowly tailored to meet its diversity objective. As a result, the Supreme Court remanded to the Fifth Circuit. In so doing, the Court set out three controlling principles relevant to assessing the constitutionality of a public university's affirmative-action program:

(1) Because racial characteristics so seldom provide a relevant basis for disparate treatment, [r]ace may not be considered [by a university] unless the admissions process can withstand strict scrutiny.[77]

(2) The decision to pursue "the educational benefits that flow from student body diversity" . . . is, in substantial measure,

an academic judgment to which some, but not complete, judicial deference is proper.[78]

(3) The University must prove that the means chosen by the University to attain diversity are narrowly tailored to that goal. On this point, the University receives no deference.[79]

On remand, the Fifth Circuit again upheld the university's admissions program, and in 2016 the case returned to the Supreme Court. *Fisher II* affirmed the Fifth Circuit's decision, holding that the University of Texas at Austin's undergraduate admissions policy survived strict scrutiny, in accordance with *Fisher I*. In an opinion authored by Justice Kennedy and joined by Justices Ginsburg, Breyer, and Sotomayor (with Justice Kagan recused), the Court again affirmed its support for educational diversity as a compelling state interest, singling out as expected benefits "enhanced classroom dialogue and the lessening of racial isolation and stereotypes."[80]

It is worth nothing that Kennedy's opinion rebuked Fisher's arguments that academic merit alone should be the criterion for admissions. "A system that selected every student through class rank alone would exclude the star athlete or musician whose grades suffered because of daily practices and training," he wrote. "It would exclude a talented young biologist who struggled to maintain above-average grades in humanities classes. And it would exclude a student whose freshman-year grades were poor because of a family crisis but who got herself back on track in her last three years of school." Further, Kennedy added, once "a university gives 'a reasoned, principled explanation' for its decision [to use race as a factor in admissions], deference must be given 'to the University's conclusion, based on its experience and expertise, that a diverse student body would serve its educational goals.'"[81]

But Kennedy also made clear that there must be some sort of evidentiary record indicating that the university's ambitions cannot be met by some other means. His opinion relied heavily on empirical evidence showing that the alternative considerations and programming done by the university failed to reach the stated goal of diversity. The opinion is grounded in factual analysis of admissions procedure, not vague theoretical considerations of "diversity." In other words, the high bar of strict scrutiny's "narrow tailoring" was met because viable alternatives were not feasible.

Kennedy closed the opinion on a mixed note for supporters of affirmative action. While his opinion reaffirmed *Grutter* and upheld the Texas system, he did not give carte blanche to affirmative action policies, writing, "The Court's affirmance of the University's admissions policy today does not necessarily mean the University may rely on that same policy without refinement. It is the University's ongoing obligation to engage in constant deliberation and continued reflection regarding its admissions policies."[82]

WHAT'S NEXT?

By the time the *Fisher II* ruling was issued in the summer of 2016, a new chapter had begun in the story about race in America, one unmatched in terms of contentiousness—and at times combustibility—since the height of the civil rights era. The Black Lives Matter movement, formed in 2013 in response to a police murder in Ferguson, Missouri, was growing quickly and asserting itself. The scandal of Black incarceration rates was put squarely before the American public's eyes. In 2014 journalist and author Ta-Nehisi Coates published an influential article titled "The Case for Reparations," which focused on redlining and housing discrimination directed at Black Americans and the devastating effects of such practices. Moreover, President Donald Trump inflamed race relations with his frequent and divisive race-baiting and callousness, especially in the aftermath of the 2017 "Unite the Right" rally in Charlottesville, Virginia. In 2020 George Floyd's murder repulsed and outraged the world. By 2021 the U.S. Congress was reopening discussion and study of reparations for Black Americans.[83]

Though scholarly constitutional rationalizations for affirmative action were overshadowed in public discourse by other racial matters, the topic, necessarily, remained a major priority among our colleagues in higher education and to applicants—especially since President Trump had higher education in his sights. Indeed, in 2018 the Trump administration ordered the rolling back of several Obama-era guidelines promoting the use of race as a factor in college admissions, calling for a "race-neutral" admissions process instead.[84] Accordingly, between *Bakke* and the present, about twenty major affirmative action disputes have commanded the attention of admissions officers, civil rights advocates, libertarians, voters and jurists in cases that ascended to the federal courts and the high court, as well as in ballot initiatives introduced in various state legislatures that copied Proposition 209.[85]

Against this backdrop, two lawsuits, in particular, have come to the fore: *Students for Fair Admissions v. Harvard* and *Students for Fair Admissions v. University of North Carolina at Chapel Hill*. The cases, both filed in 2014, have for almost a decade been making their way through the courts. They present the most serious challenge to forty years of established legal precedent allowing colleges to consider the race of applicants in admissions in order to promote the benefits of diverse learning environments. The two cases, which we address in detail in Chapter 4, represent opposite sides of the same coin: The Harvard case contends that undergraduate Asian

American applicants to Harvard were denied admission on the basis of their race. Alternatively, the UNC plaintiffs maintain that UNC impermissibly favors Black and Hispanic students over others (including Asian American and white students).

Once again, then, the so-called diversity in education rationale initiated by Powell in *Bakke,* which has been unhelpfully vague and counterproductive in addressing the underlying realities of systemic racism in America, will be robustly debated. As will the Court's interpretation of the Fourteenth Amendment, which has implications for the UNC case because it is a publicly funded state university (as opposed to Harvard's status as a private institution). Critics of affirmative action will contend that under no circumstances should the state be permitted to take race into account—even with the best intentions—because empowering the government to make exceptions to that prohibition for ostensibly good reasons can result in abuses by that same government for bad reasons.

We disagree. We believe good judgment can be—and has in the past been—exercised and that the rewards of making carefully considered exceptions outweigh the risks of absolute prohibition against them. Further, we, along with many other legal scholars, contend that the "originalist" interpretation of the Fourteenth Amendment leaves room for factoring in race as a consideration. Indeed, when it comes to its interpretation, the language is unambiguous: "No State shall . . . deny to any person within its jurisdiction the equal protection of the laws."[86] Many legal scholars contend that, far from establishing a constitutional ban on any consideration of race, the framers of the Fourteenth Amendment enacted a broad, universal *guarantee of equality.* In so doing, the framers expressly rejected proposed constitutional language that would have prohibited race-conscious efforts to achieve equal protection. Further underscoring the framers' intent to enact a comprehensive guarantee of equality, they simultaneously passed a "long list of race-conscious legislation to help ensure that the Amendment's promise of equality would be a reality for African Americans."[87]

This scholarship provides a strong justification for affirmative action, particularly for those who place emphasis on the original intention of the framers when considering constitutional issues.[88]

A compelling example of how this legal theory has been applied in concrete terms is the Bureau of Refugees, Freedmen, and Abandoned Lands—colloquially known as the Freedmen's Bureau—a government agency established in 1865 to assist former slaves in the wake of the Civil War. The bureau "provided its charges with clothing, food, fuel, and medicine; it built, staffed, and operated their schools and hospitals; it wrote their leases and their labor contracts, [and] rented them land."[89] Though the bureau aided both freed slaves and wartime refugees of any race, it explicitly granted additional benefits to freed slaves: The bureau, as expanded by additional legislation in 1866, was authorized to "aid" them in any manner "in making the freedom conferred by proclamation of the commander in chief, by emancipation under the laws of States, and by constitutional amendment," while providing support to "loyal refugees" only to the extent "the same shall be necessary to enable them . . . to become self-supporting citizens."[90] Other legislation passed during the Reconstruction era also expressly benefited Black Americans, regardless of whether those individuals were newly freed slaves or not. For example, Congress established a bank, the Freedman's Savings and Trust Company, for "persons heretofore held in slavery in the United States or their descendants."[91] In 1866 it also appropriated money "for the 'National association for the relief of destitute colored women and children,'[92] "for the purpose of supporting . . . aged or indigent and destitute colored women and children."[93] These explicit references to race, in legislation enacted simultaneous with the Fourteenth Amendment, render undeniable what the text of that amendment already made clear: in passing the Fourteenth Amendment, the framers did not intend to foreclose any governmental reliance on race for any reason.[94]

In short, the lens through which the most persistent opponents of affirmative action continue to view the Fourteenth Amendment is distorted: It is not an either/or proposition, a choice between equal treatment under the law or considerations of race—it is *both*.

Half a century after President Kennedy signed the executive order on affirmative action, the policy faces new challenges. On one hand, there is a pervasive feeling, especially among Black citizens and increasingly among white people, that injustice has for too long been ignored, slighted, or denied, and that we must insist on a discussion that is uninhibited, wide open, and fully accountable to the past. On the other hand, the *Students for Fair Admissions* cases do not exclusively pit Black students against white students in a zero-sum-game admissions contest; instead, this latest contest is between historically oppressed minority groups, which adds a new layer of complexity to the debate over the long-term viability and validity of affirmative action.

The Unfinished Journey

The State of Race in American Society Today

Many Americans are anxious to believe that their country has leveled the playing field and delivered equal opportunity to its Black citizens, but wide educational, economic, and social gaps between Black and white citizens remain. Indeed, in the decades since *Brown v. Board of Education*, the civil rights movement, and the advent of affirmative action, American society has become, in many respects, *more* racially stratified than it was a half century ago.

We acknowledge that many Black Americans have made progress. Nonetheless, we contend that the United States remains, essentially, two separate spheres: one Black, the other white.

Laws may compel individuals and institutions to change their behavior, but they cannot compel those same individuals and institutions to change their attitudes. The law's reach extends only so far. The hearts, minds, and customs of a nation are forged and ingrained—and in the case of race relations in America, have been hardened to the point of calcification—over the course of centuries. Though the process can be slow, messy, and contentious, passing legislation and issuing court rulings is actually the easy part: It is far more difficult to unlearn bias. This is a much slower undertaking.

And since the beginning of the civil rights project, there has never been congruence between efforts to eradicate de jure and de facto discrimination. Changes in laws and legislation have preceded changes in public attitudes and behaviors in nearly every instance. This is why we reject the premise that just because de jure discrimination against Black citizens was outlawed, white America now has permission to conclude that the nation's journey for racial justice is, if not completed entirely, advancing admirably and steadily. If such were indeed the case, then why is it that nearly seven decades into this project, we are nowhere near the fully integrated, fully equal society we sought to create?

Since the 1960, large swaths of white America may have supported integration in principle but, in practice, maintained a distance— literally and figuratively, consciously and unconsciously—from their Black countrymen and -women. For just as water rolling down a mountain is not stopped by the boulder but simply maneuvers around it, white America, after *Brown*, executed its own "workaround." De facto discrimination continued, and continues to this day. Many Black and white Americans remain separated by geography, social class, careers, incomes, educational attainment, and access to social and financial services.

A cohort of Americans, particularly those who live in urban milieus, may today take pride in the rich diversity that envelops them. And, indeed, in our major cities, it is possible to walk down a street and encounter people of almost every conceivable race or ethnicity. But does this truly reflect the end of racial separation and discrimination? Especially when, in many of these same cities, certain sections of town are still designated by residents as Black neighborhoods? Further, with rare exceptions, travel is conducted in a one-way direction: Far more Black Americans venture into, and onto, white America's social and economic "turf" than vice versa.

Many white Americans may, on an intellectual level, support racial equality. But, as a matter of deeply ingrained habit, most white Americans still perceive and interact with Black Americans as "the other," socially, culturally, economically, politically and professionally.

The playing fields on which Black and white Americans compete—which in the 1950s and 1960s were ostensibly merged—remain in many respects separate and unequal. And, although the law may no longer discriminate against Black citizens, money and power still can—*and do.* The forms in which this discrimination occurs can be conspicuous or inconspicuous. The most conspicuous expression occurs in the criminal justice system, and it deservedly commands an outsized share of public attention, given its life-or-death implications. Less conspicuous, but still pernicious, is the discrimination Black Americans continue to experience across almost every facet of life: in healthcare, housing, access to capital, employment, civic participation, and, notably, education.

To better understand where we are today and how we got here, let us once again rewind the clock.

Since 1967, things have changed for the better, to be sure. In 1968 one in three Black Americans lived in poverty; today the number has declined to one in five.[1] Since 1968, Black Americans' inflation-adjusted annual household income has increased by 43 percent.[2] Nine in ten Black students graduate from high school today, compared to about five in ten in the late 1960s.[3] In 2008 the nation elected its first Black president, Barack Obama, and three racial minorities are represented on the Supreme Court.

There is still considerable room for improvement, however.

IN CONTEMPORARY AMERICA, HOUSING REMAINS SEPARATE AND UNEQUAL

In the private sphere, housing discrimination against Black Americans has a long and disgraceful past, one dating back centuries. The country had an opportunity to redress these injustices in 1934, when the Roosevelt administration established the Federal Housing Administration. Faced with a housing shortage, the government began a program to increase supply—mostly in suburbs. But Black Americans' hopes of achieving equal access to housing were soon dashed: The federal housing programs initiated under the New Deal were tantamount to a "state-sponsored system of segregation." The government's efforts were "primarily designed to provide housing to white, middle-class, lower-middle-class families." Black Americans were excluded, and instead steered into urban housing projects, reports Richard Rothstein, author of *The Color of Law*.[4]

As we discussed earlier, the G.I. Bill presented another opportunity to redress past wrongs but, once again, failed Black citizens. As a 2020 article from the Brookings Institution[5] reported: "After World War II, loans guaranteed by the Federal Housing Administration and the Department of Veterans Affairs opened up the possibility of homeownership (and wealth-building) to millions of American households. However, these loan programs were explicitly structured to exclude Black citizens and to favor particular places: the newly minted suburbs."[6] Indeed, Black homeownership has never achieved parity with white homeownership. By 1968, almost twenty years into a postwar economic boom that transformed the United States into the world's richest country,[7] 65 percent of white Americans owned their homes[8] compared to 40 percent of Black Americans—a rate virtually unchanged since.[9]

In 1954 *Brown* sought to integrate schools. But what *Brown* did not anticipate was that many white people would rather flee from communities co-inhabited by Black citizens than mix with them. Nor did *Brown* anticipate that as white residents fled cities, the tax dollars necessary for maintaining infrastructure, providing quality medical services, operating quality schools, and delivering fair and affordable housing would exit with them. From the 1950s onward, many corporations—and jobs—left major downtown metropolitan areas. Thus began a domino effect in major cities, because, when the white people left they took businesses with them. In 1960, more than six in ten U.S. jobs were in cities; by 1996 those rates had plunged to a mere 16 percent.[10] Consider Atlanta, which could just as easily stand in for Chicago, Detroit, and other major cities. In 1960 downtown Atlanta accounted for 90 percent of the region's office space; by 1980, that figure was 42 percent; by 1999, just 13 percent.[11]

Millions of Black Americans continue to reckon with the impact of white America's hasty exit. The Kerner Report highlighted the dual phenomenon of a post-*Brown* white exodus and Black inmigration into northern cities from the South, which translated into more Black residents and fewer white ones in urban areas. Between 1940 and 1970, four million Black people left the South, increasing the Black population in northern and western cities from 4 percent in 1940 to 16 percent in 1970. To get a sense of how dramatic the transformation of the urban landscape was, and how quickly it occurred, consider that in 1950, the fifty largest metropolitan areas contained almost half of the country's population, and these areas, in the aggregate, were 90 percent white (matching the nation's demographics as a whole). According to the Kerner Report, "45.5 million whites lived in central cities. If this population had grown from 1950 to 1960 at the same rate as the nation's white population as a whole, it would have increased by 8 million. Instead, it rose only 2.2 million, indicating an outflow of 5.8 million whites."[12]

And the whites were not keen to allow Black Americans to follow them to the suburbs. When open-housing laws outlawed discriminatory advertising and lending practices, realtors and landlords cried foul. They claimed that their clients and tenants had a right to live among those whose company they preferred, citing as justification their First Amendment right to associate freely with whomever they chose. In 1964 the voters of California agreed, and repealed the state's fair-housing laws by a two-to-one margin.[13]

For Black Americans left behind to fend for themselves in urban centers, the prognosis was not good. Some cities that white people fled became urban husks, replete with grinding poverty, crime, uncollected trash, abandoned residential buildings, and boarded-up storefronts. A quarter century after building the first federal public housing project, Techwood Homes in Atlanta, Georgia, in 1935, a 604-unit whites-only apartment complex that displaced hundreds of Black residents, who were evicted from the land,[14] the public housing projects of the 1950s and 1960s were initiated. Low-income Black citizens, many of whom had grown up in the rural South, were steered into such high-rise apartment buildings as the Robert Taylor Homes and Cabrini Green in Chicago, the Jordan Downs Housing Projects of Watts, the Magnolia Projects of New Orleans, and the Pruitt–Igoe housing projects in St. Louis.

During the 1950s and 1960s, as the nation fixed its gaze on the South—on National Guardsmen escorting Black girls into schools in Arkansas and on Bull Connor and his dogs in Alabama—few in the North and West were similarly attentive to the grim conditions under which racial minorities in their own backyards lived. From New York's Harlem to Chicago's South Side, to Watts and other Black neighborhoods in and around Los Angeles, postwar population density increased significantly, but the boundaries of those communities, overcrowded, overpriced and unsafe, remained fixed. In these areas, landlords refused to invest in leaky, at times rat-infested properties and grocery chains refused to open stores, creating food deserts where not much beyond overpriced junk food was available.[15] Accordingly, the urban Black communities of the North and the West, long simmering quietly, were reaching a boiling point of their own by the mid-1960s. Between 1964 and 1968, 329 major riots occurred in 257 northern and western cities, the pent-up rage taking expression in the Black neighborhoods of Chicago, Detroit, Cleveland, Los Angeles, and Newark, among others, including medium-sized and small cities with populations of fewer than fifty thousand residents.[16] It is worth noting that the riots were limited to Black-majority neighborhoods: Rage was not directed at white people in suburbs or at major governmental, business, or civic institutions, but at the dire conditions *inside* Black communities.

In 1967 President Johnson convened what would become known as the Kerner Commission (named after its chair, Illinois governor Otto Kerner) to determine the root cause of the social unrest and to identify policy solutions moving forward. The rioters' key grievances, the commission concluded, were the police—who applied "indiscriminate use of force against wholly innocent elements of the Negro community" during the riots—and white-owned businesses operating in the communities.[17,] "What the rioters appeared to be seeking," concluded the Kerner Commission, "was fuller participation in the social order and the material benefits enjoyed by the majority of American citizens. Rather than rejecting the American system, they were anxious to obtain a place for themselves in it." In short, the rioters were not keen to tear down American society; they were pleading *to be let in.*[18] The commission concluded, "What white Americans have never fully understood but what the Negro can never forget, is that white society is deeply implicated in the ghetto. White institutions created it, white institutions maintain it, and white society condones it."[19]

Nearly all the major urban conflagrations of the mid-1960s began as an altercation between Black residents and white police officers. This pattern held true for the following decades.

A dramatic example of this occurred on August 9, 2014, when Michael Brown, a Black teenager in Ferguson, Missouri, a suburb of St. Louis, was shot by white police officer Darren Wilson. A day later, protests erupted, and the unrest continued for the next four months.[20] While the protests after Michael Brown's death focused, rightly, on the relations between law enforcement officers and Black Americans, in Ferguson there was another story behind the headline-generating one. Indeed, St. Louis's—and Ferguson's—story of white flight and re-segregation was a smoldering tinder box decades in the making.

The City of St. Louis, situated at the confluence of the Mississippi and Missouri Rivers, is not very large—about sixty-five square miles in total.[21] After the interstate highway systems commissioned by President Eisenhower were laid, it became possible to drive from the northernmost part of the city to its southernmost part in about twenty minutes. The drive from the easternmost part of the city, beneath the famous Gateway Arch, to the city's westernmost edge was even shorter—about ten minutes, if traffic was light. Until well into the twentieth century, the area north, south, and west of the city proper comprised suburbs and farmland contained in a separately incorporated entity, St. Louis County. In 1960 the total population of the City of St. Louis numbered 750,026 residents, of whom seven in ten were white and three in ten were Black.[22] Then, like hundreds of other U.S. cities, white residents fled to the suburbs. They migrated in three directions: The more affluent professional classes moved to western St. Louis County, whereas the working-class migrants relocated to southern St. Louis County and northern St. Louis County, which included the blue-collar township of Ferguson.[23]

As St. Louis's Black middle class grew in the late 1960s and 1970s, Black residents keen to exit the city also migrated to the northern townships, including Ferguson, which, in 1970, was 99 percent white. Shortly after Black residents' arrival, FOR SALE signs soon appeared in some white residents' yards. By 1980, 86 percent of Ferguson's residents were white; by 1990, 75 percent were white; by 2000, 48 percent were white; and by 2010, 33 percent were white.[24]

Fifty years on, the City of St. Louis's urban population, 301,578, is less than half what it was in 1970. Inside the city limits, the population is 46 percent Black, 46 percent white, and 8 percent other— but this does not mean that, on a block-by-block basis, this level of integration exists.

The story of St. Louis's resegregation is the nation's story. And geographical segregation by race is a two-sided coin, with low-income Black citizens living in predominantly Black neighborhoods and upper-income Black citizens living in predominantly Black neighborhoods, too, from coast to coast. As *Black Enterprise* magazine reports, many of Los Angeles's affluent Black residents live in the suburbs of Ladera Heights and View Park–Windsor Hills, a community dubbed "Black Beverly Hills" because 75 percent of the community's inhabitants are Black.[25] Eight miles away is Beverly Hills, which is 81 percent white and less than 2 percent Black.[26] On the opposite side of the country, leafy Bethesda, Maryland, home to affluent Washingtonians, is 78 percent white and less than 5 percent Black.[27] Yet only a half hour's drive away can be found the Maryland suburbs of Woodmore, Kettering, and Mitchellville, where household incomes are high, home values are high, and educational levels are high—and 70 to 85 percent of the residents are Black, depending on the town.[28] Further, in contravention of the Fair Housing Act, many prospective Black renters and homeowners keen to settle in white-majority neighborhoods are discouraged from doing so. As recently as 2019, investigative journalists from *Newsday* revealed that real estate agents in Long Island were steering white clients into white neighborhoods and minority clients into lower-income minority neighborhoods.[29]

Most unwelcome in suburbs are affordable housing developments. In 2021 *Vox* published a survey of 1,116 likely voters nationwide on their attitudes about housing. Six in ten likely voters said they wanted the government to build affordable housing—but not in their backyards.[30] Indeed, despite court rulings and laws intended to remedy housing segregation, for decades, from coast to coast, wealthy, majority-white communities have routinely erected invisible walls to affordable housing. For example, an investigation conducted jointly by the *Connecticut Mirror* and *ProPublica*, which produces investigative journalism in the public interest, reported that, statewide, "many zoning boards rely on their finely tuned regulations to keep housing segregation firmly in place. They point to frail public infrastructure, clogged streets, a lack of sidewalks and concerns of overcrowding that would damage what's often referred to as 'neighborhood character.' "[31] The investigation noted that over the course of the preceding three decades, of the twenty-seven thousand affordable housing units in Connecticut—whose construction was funded by almost $2.2 billion in low-income housing tax credits—eight in ten had been built in struggling communities.[32] Further down the East Coast, in Montgomery County, Maryland, one of the most affluent counties in the United States,[33] advocates' appeals to create affordable housing in 2021 were likewise greeted with resistance. A community letter signed by 197 residents of

Silver Spring's Woodside Park neighborhood and presented to the County Council, claimed that new housing designed for middle- and low-income newcomers would "'deeply undermine the character, natural assets, and future stability' of the neighborhood."[34]

Jim Crow–era policies dictating where Black Americans could or could not live may have been overturned by courts, but they morphed into state laws and local ordinances that continue to allow landlords to determine where low-income Black residents— especially Section 8 voucher holders who receive rental housing assistance paid to private landlords on their behalf—can live.[35] Federal law does not prevent landlords from rejecting housing vouchers, with limited exceptions. As *Vox* reported, in major cities from Los Angeles to New York to Philadelphia to Chicago, voucher holders often encounter landlords who refuse to take them or find other ways to avoid renting to them, including falsely claiming that they have no available apartments.[36] And though some states and localities have prohibited discrimination against families that use housing vouchers, only one in three households that use vouchers are protected by such laws.[37]

Discrimination against voucher holders remains common, as the Urban Institute reported in a 2018 study. To determine its extent, the organization's researchers called thousands of landlords in five cities, all of whom were listing voucher-eligible apartments. "Rejection rates were higher in lower-poverty neighborhoods, suggesting that voucher holders who want to find housing in an 'opportunity' area—perhaps close to high-quality schools, jobs, and transportation—will face even more rejection," the report's authors concluded.[38]

Further, among low-income Black Americans, housing struggles have actually intensified in recent years. During the Great Recession of 2007–2009, for example, when unemployment soared to 16.8

percent for Black workers, Black families endured the highest rates of foreclosure and lost the most wealth. Homeownership never fully rebounded in these communities.[39] Perhaps the most damning statistic of all: Despite comprising just 13 percent of the total U.S. population, Black Americans account for 40 percent of America's homeless population.[40]

IN CONTEMPORARY AMERICA, EDUCATION REMAINS SEPARATE AND UNEQUAL

Since the central argument in this book is that affirmative action for Black students in higher education remains vital and necessary, let us now turn to the phenomenon of school resegregation, which began almost immediately after the *Brown* decision.

Between the nation's founding and 1954, Black and white school children, with rare exceptions, were educated separately. Then, between, roughly 1955 until the conclusion of the busing controversies of the 1970s, millions of white and Black students sat side by side in integrated classrooms. To be sure, many parents resisted integration, and for two decades television screens across the nation flickered with images of Black children being escorted into elementary schools by national guardsmen or of angry white parents staging protests at school bus stops. And millions of white children in urban areas were evacuated by their parents to the suburbs just to avoid being coeducated with Black children. Nonetheless, millions of white Americans' children, beginning with the generation born after 1965, which would become known as Generation X, entered integrated public schools. On the first day of school, these children—Black children, white children, and, in-creasingly, Latinx and other minority students—simply took their seats, as the teacher instructed, and sat together in class for the next thirteen years, participating in recess, gym class, and sports, and in clubs together. During the 1970s and 1980s, public schools added acknowledgment of America's shameful treatment of its Black citizens to school curricula. Students were instructed about the legacy of slavery, about segregation, Jim Crow and *Brown's* determination to eradicate it; students watched the horrific videos of Bull Connor and his attack dogs in civics class; they sat with their families in front of the television in the mid-1970s and watched *Roots*, the miniseries based on Alex Haley's 1976 novel about chattel slavery in America, which would become one of the most widely viewed programs in television history. Thirty-five years after *Brown*, 1989 was identified by the UCLA Civil Rights Project as the highwater mark for school-integration success. In that year 44 percent of Black students in the South attended schools that were at least 50 percent white.[41]

But then—either unexpectedly or predictably, depending on one's point of view about race relations in America—by the late 1980s, a pernicious form of de facto resegregation began to reappear in the form of private K-12 schools. Over the course of a quarter century, from 1988 to 2014, the number of public K-12 schools in the United States that had a 99 percent nonwhite student population tripled, from 2,762 schools to 6,727.[42] The numbers in one school district are particularly distressing: In 1968 white students accounted for about 54 percent of the student population of Houston's Independent School District; by the early 2000s, white students represented less than 10 percent.[43] And the drop in white enrollment is not limited to Texas; by the 2010s, the percentage of Black students attending schools across the American South that were at least 50 percent white plunged by nearly half to 23 percent.[44]

A key driver of resegregation and inequality is the local property tax, which ensures that all public schools are not funded equally.

Egregious disparities in per-pupil expenditures exist in this country on an interstate level and at the intra-district level. To that end, a half century ago, a group of low-income parents asserted that Texas's public education financing system violated the Fourteenth Amendment's Equal Protection Clause by failing to distribute funding equally among its school districts. Their lawsuit, *San Antonio Independent School District v. Rodriguez*,[45] eventually ascended to the Supreme Court and, in 1973, the bitterly divided Court, in a 5–4 ruling, held that the school district's financing system was not an unconstitutional violation of the Equal Protection Clause because disparities in school funding were not intended to harm racial minorities and, further, education was not a fundamental right protected by the Constitution.[46]

This decision has the dubious honor of regularly appearing on lists of the worst Supreme Court rulings in history, alongside *Dred Scott, Plessy,* and *Korematsu v. United States,* which upheld the detention of more than 110,000 Japanese-Americans during World War II.[47]

The legacy of this decision is felt today in the gerrymandering of school districts, which has become increasingly common. In such cities as Birmingham, Alabama, to cite just one example, instead of moving or enrolling their children in private or specialized public schools, many wealthy, predominantly white families have opted out of integrated schools by supporting the secession of their neighborhoods from larger school districts.[48]

As expected, the re-emergence of separate K-12 educational facilities has created unequal outcomes for Black and white students in America. Urban school systems, whose student bodies are made up disproportionately of minorities, remain underfunded. Students are often instructed by less-qualified teachers who are paid lower salaries than those in white-majority suburban schools.[49] One study found that predominantly white school districts, collectively, receive $23 billion more per year than predominantly nonwhite school districts.[50] Further, as the United Negro College Fund, an American philanthropic organization that funds scholarships for Black students, reports, they are less likely than white students to have access to college-preparatory-level math and science courses. In 2011, for example, 57 percent of Black students had access to such courses compared to 71 percent of white students and 81 percent of Asian American students. Further, Black students are subject to systematic bias in teacher expectations, with non-Black teachers expressing lower expectations of Black students than do Black teachers. Black students, who are disciplined disproportionately compared to white students, spend less time in the classroom, thus reducing their access to a quality education.[51]

The divide today is as much economic as it is racial, because predominantly Black or Hispanic schools have a higher concentration of students in poverty.[52] Indeed, in almost all major American cities, most Black and Hispanic students attend public schools where a majority of their classmates qualify as poor or low-income, as an analysis of federal data shows.[53]

As a result, Black Americans still lag behind white Americans in overall educational attainment, resulting in higher average 2021 SAT test scores for white students (1,112) than Black students (934)[54] and, alternatively, higher school dropout rates for Black males, who are twice as likely to quit school as their white male classmates.[55]

Most Americans acknowledge that fundamentally resegregated K-12 public schools are not delivering equal outcomes for children. They know that majority-Black and Latinx schools are underfunded, understaffed, and substandard vis-à-vis majority-white schools. Most Americans will be distressed, but few, in our opinion, will be surprised, to learn that the average Black student who has completed his or her thirteen-year journey through the K-12 education system in America is, on average, half as college-ready as other students. For example, the ACT exam includes four "college readiness" benchmarks. In 2015, six in ten Black students who took the exam met none of the benchmarks.[56] It is frustrating that most Americans have also watched—for decades—as politicians, school boards, teachers' unions, and others have struggled to fix the gross inequities inherent in our nation's educational system, with nominal success.

Which brings us to Black student matriculation into colleges and universities, for it is this milieu, perhaps more than any other, that functions as Black Americans' passport to upward economic and social mobility. Conditions may have been separate and unequal in K-12, but, ostensibly, once enrolled in a college or university, Black America's "best and brightest" can ascend.

But the journey into higher education presents a steep climb for most Black students, both academically and financially. Among those fortunate enough to enroll in a college or university, too many arrive underprepared vis-à-vis white and Asian students. While we are pleased to see that more African Americans gain a college diploma today than during the civil rights era—an increase from just 4 percent in 1962 to 26 percent in 2019[57]—as the authors of "50 Years After the Kerner Commission," a report issued by the Economic Policy Institute, recently noted: "In 1968 blacks were just over half as likely as whites to have a college degree, a situation that is essentially the same today."[58]

And, distressingly, students of color, especially Black and Latinx students, remain underrepresented at selective universities.[59] In fact, a disparity in Black student enrollment exists at forty-five of the fifty flagship state universities.[60] In other words, the percentage of undergraduates who are Black is lower than the percentage of high school graduates in that state who are Black. In fifteen of the fifty states, the public universities had at least a ten-point gap.[61] In Mississippi, 50 percent of high school students are Black, but as recently as 2016, only 13 percent were members of the undergraduate population at the University of Mississippi.[62] And those who exit with a diploma will also carry a higher debt burden than their white classmates. According to the Brookings Institution, four years after graduation, the average Black college graduate owes $52,726, in student loan debt compared to $28,006 for the average white college graduate.[63]

IN CONTEMPORARY AMERICA, HEALTHCARE ACCESS AND OUTCOMES REMAIN SEPARATE AND UNEQUAL

The Century Foundation, in a 2019 report titled "Racism, Inequality, and Health Care for African Americans," stated the problem bluntly: "Place matters." As the report states: "Often, people of color find themselves relying heavily on community health centers, emergency rooms or outpatient care, and community-based providers due to the lack of available primary care and mental health providers in a given geographic area," the report stated. "Traveling outside of the immediate geographic area to access health care may be an option for some people, yet this can be a challenge due to lack of access to transportation for those with limited incomes or for those living in rural areas."[64]

Further, Black Americans typically pay more for medical care and incur more medical debt. "The average American family spends $8,200 annually—or 11 percent of family income—on health care premiums, and out-of-pocket costs," according to the Century

Foundation report. "For Black Americans, the average annual cost for health care premiums is almost 20 percent of the average household income—a major cost to bear, when taking into account income inequality and other economic challenges for this demographic."[65] Black patients incur a higher level of medical debt (defined as greater than 20 percent of yearly household income) than white people—27 percent of Black households hold medical debt compared to 17 percent of non-Black households—which, in turn, discourages preventative and therapeutic treatments and increases the risk of future acute health problems.[66]

All of this leads to separate and unequal healthcare outcomes. Across the board, Black Americans experience the highest rates of obesity,[67] hypertension,[68] maternal mortality, infant mortality,[69] stroke,[70] and asthma.[71] Black men, in particular, do not have promising long-term health prognoses: They have lower five-year cancer survival rates than do white men and are twice as likely to die from prostate cancer as white men.[72] The Covid pandemic, in particular, brought these disparities into sharp relief: Black Americans contracted and died from Covid at higher rates than white Americans.[73] In 2021, two years into the Covid pandemic, the CDC reported that Black Americans lost three years of life expectancy due to Covid.[74] Further, their access to the most sustaining aspect of life, food, is likewise unequal, because they experience hunger at twice the rate of white Americans, including one in four Black children.[75]

Finally, and most devastating, there is one public health statistic affecting the Black community to which too many Americans have become numbed: According to a 2019 CDC report, Black men and boys aged fifteen to thirty-four—who comprise just 2 percent of the nation's population—represented 37 percent of gun homicide victims that year, twenty times higher than white males of the same age group.[76]

IN CONTEMPORARY AMERICA, BLACK AMERICANS' OPPORTUNITY TO ACCRUE WEALTH AND ACHIEVE FINANCIAL SECURITY REMAINS SEPARATE AND UNEQUAL

Across virtually every financial metric, Black Americans lag behind their white counterparts. From a disadvantaged starting point at the very back of the line—where for centuries they were denied access to financial services, bank loans, jobs, pay parity, participation in profit-sharing schemes and retirement funds, and so on—Black Americans have made progress, but they have still not caught up to White America.

While it is true that, since 1968, the Black poverty rate has been reduced substantially, and about one in three Black Americans say their personal financial situation is either in excellent or good shape, compared with one in two U.S. adults overall,[77] among Black Americans, wealth accrual varies sharply by educational attainment. Today, nearly half of Black households are unbanked or underbanked, a disparity that, over the course of a financial lifetime, can cost Black consumers nearly $40,000 in fees.[78] Even something as ostensibly easy as opening and maintaining a basic checking and savings account is unequal. Banks have a larger footprint in white communities than Black communities; Black customers incur higher banking fees. Black individuals and families, as a result, must either supplement conventional banking methods or perhaps replace them with alternatives: check-cashing services, payday loans, money orders, and prepaid credit cards.[79] As the National Fair Housing Alliance has reported, these services are often delivered to Black consumers with a catch: exorbitant fees and interest rates. It has been shown that minority car shoppers who are demonstrably more qualified than their white counterparts are 62.5 percent more likely to be offered costlier pricing options, adding up to $2,662 in extra fees and interest over the life of the loan.[80]

Nor has there been much movement in the disparity between the wages of Black and white Americans: Black households bring home two-thirds the earnings of white households, and this disparity has barely changed over the past fifty years. The combination of being paid lower salaries than white people and being forced to pay higher fees and interest rates hampers the prospect of long-term wealth-building. Not surprisingly, the wealth gap between Black and white Americans is wide—and it is growing.[81] As of 2016, the net worth of the average Black American family was about one-tenth that of their white counterparts: $17,600 and $171,000, respectively.[82] Moreover, Black Americans were 2.5 times as likely to be in poverty as white Americans.[83]

The gap in retirement savings is notably stark: Among the 60 percent of white Americans who own retirement accounts, their balances are, on average, $77,000; among the 34 percent of Black Americans who own retirement accounts, the balance is one-third as much, or $24,600.[84] And the Covid-19 pandemic only made things worse for many Black families who, in the face of layoffs, pay cuts, and reductions in hours, were, as the Center for American Progress reported in the summer of 2021, "less likely than white households to have savings and . . . often ended up borrowing money from family and friends to pay for current expenses."[85]

It is heartening that, since the mid-1970s, Black unemployment has been halved.[86] By 2019, Black Americans accounted for 12 percent of the U.S. workforce,[87] almost matching their 13 percent representation in the general population[88]. Still, over approximately the same time period, the Black unemployment rate has consistently been about twice the white unemployment rate: 13 percent for Black Americans in 2020 and about 7 percent for white Americans.[89] Further, the gap between median earnings of Black men and white men remains unchanged since the 1950s.[90]

In the pages of this book, we have been determined to rebut the argument that, because our universities now mint Black PhDs, Black Americans now occupy high ranks in our leading institutions, and America can now boast that it has seven Black billionaires,[91] Black citizens enjoy equal access to the American Dream. But many Black Americans—millions, in fact—are so vastly under-resourced that their best hope is simply to stay afloat financially, to avoid sinking further into poverty. By all means, we should hold up inspirational high-achieving Black Americans as role models. But we must, in addition to looking up, continue to look out, across the *entire* Black American landscape, at what for many is a brutal daily grind, one rife with financial insecurity. Because, for every billionaire media mogul like Oprah Winfrey, billionaire sports legend like Michael Jordan, or billionaire entertainer like Jay-Z, Kanye West, or Tyler Perry, or investor Robert F. Smith (the richest Black man in the country, with a net worth of nearly $7 billion),[92] the average Black family in America has merely five days of liquid savings on hand.[93]

IN CONTEMPORARY AMERICA, BLACK AMERICANS' OPPORTUNITIES TO ASCEND IN THE WORKPLACE REMAIN SEPARATE AND UNEQUAL

Discrimination against Black job candidates has not been eradicated. Title VII of the Civil Rights Act of 1964 may have *prohibited* employment discrimination, but *proving* discrimination was far more difficult. In the unlikely event that a discrimination case made its way to court, a white defendant was far more likely to claim that he passed on the prospective Black employee because the job candidate "lacked the necessary qualifications," which could be so subjective as to be unprovable, than to bluntly admit his aversion to hiring Black people for certain positions.[94]

A recent *Harvard Business Review* article went so far as to declare that hiring discrimination against Black Americans has not declined in a quarter century. One way in which ongoing discrimination is exposed is through "résumé audits." Civil rights advocates will send two fictitious résumés to prospective employers, either via traditional mail or online. Both résumés contain equivalent qualifications. But ethnically identifiable names are chosen and submitted, and candidates with "Black-sounding" names, research has shown, are less likely to be invited to interview for positions. Civil rights advocates have also conducted in-person audits with trained pairs of testers, white and nonwhite, who both apply for the same job. By examining the rates of callbacks or invitations to job interviews, for equally credentialed white and nonwhite applicants, these studies reveal discrimination in hiring.[95] Further, as more human resource functions are turned to artificial intelligence and other, ostensibly, colorblind recruiting strategies—such as combing through professional networking platforms like LinkedIn—bias has been shown, again, to reveal itself. This may have something to do with the fact that 95 percent of the people who write software code are non-Black.[96]

Today, Black executives still remain underrepresented in the upper ranks of major businesses. Were it not for affirmative action policies, most of which began in earnest in the 1970s and 1980s, few Black executives, we contend, would ever have ascended to senior chairs. And still not enough of those chairs are occupied by Black citizens: Today, among America's professional classes, Black men and women still comprise less than 8 percent of the overall white-collar workforce and a mere 3 percent of the executive or senior leadership ranks.[97] In the history of the Fortune 500 list there have been only 19 Black CEOs out of a total of 1,800. Currently, among Fortune 500 companies, less than 1 percent—four CEOs out of 500—are Black.[98] While Black Americans are being hired by Fortune 500s with greater frequency, less notice is paid to is *where they land* inside those corporations. Most major corporations now issue annual "Social Responsibility" reports touting their institutions' diversity metrics. In most cases, such reports disclose the number of Black employees and executives on staff, but less frequently reported are detailed breakdowns regarding the seats they occupy.

As executives in publicly traded corporations are acutely aware, the path to the CEO's chair is shortest for the "Money Men" (they are almost always men), that is to say, division presidents with responsibility for profits and losses, chief financial officers, and others who generate profit for the firm or interact closely with Wall Street. The heads of these functions are far more likely to ascend to the CEO's chair than those who lead necessary but less financially relevant cost centers such as public relations, human resources, the legal department, and sustainability. It is telling that the Stanford Corporate Governance Research Initiative reports that inside Fortune 100 companies Black professionals account for just 1 percent of chief financial officers and 3 percent of executive leaders with profit-and-loss- responsibilities. Alternatively, Black professionals account for a comparatively high percentage of chief human resource officers and chief administration executives, thus reducing the chances that they will eventually be promoted to CEO or to a board role.[99] To their credit, in the aftermath of the George Floyd murder, many major corporations made public commitments to improve their diversity metrics. Black leaders now occupy one in ten board seats at S&P 500 companies.[100] And in 2021, Black leaders accounted for nearly one in two new board directors.[101]

IN CONTEMPORARY AMERICA, BLACK AMERICANS' TREATMENT AT THE POLLING PLACE REMAINS SEPARATE AND UNEQUAL

The story of efforts to frustrate Black Americans' efforts to vote, especially in the South, is well documented. And shameful. In the early republic, voting was generally limited to white male property holders. After the Civil War, Congress passed the Fifteenth Amendment to the Constitution, which ensured that men could not be denied the right to vote because of their race. The amendment was ratified by the states in 1870. American women were enfranchised, finally, by constitutional amendment in 1920. But a full century after 1870, at the peak of the civil rights movement, barriers to the franchise remained in many states, especially the South.

In 1964, a year before Congress passed the landmark Voting Rights Act (VRA), the U.S. Supreme Court ruled in *Reynolds v. Sims* that "since the right to exercise the franchise in a free and unimpaired manner is preservative of other basic civil and political rights, any alleged infringement of the right of citizens to vote must be carefully and meticulously scrutinized."[102] With the enactment of the VRA a year later, Congress sought to codify that principle, establishing two legislative pillars that are particularly relevant to the protection of minority voting. The first, Section 2, applies nationwide and prohibits practices that "result in a denial or abridgement of the right . . . to vote on account of race or color," creating a cause of action for plaintiffs who have been subjected to racial vote dilution or denial. The second, Section 5, applied only to the (mostly southern) jurisdictions specified by way of a formula in Section 4 of the VRA based on a record of past racial discrimination in voting. Section 5 required those "covered jurisdictions" to obtain preclearance from the federal government before making any changes in voting "practice[s] ... or procedure[s]," including redistricting, voter identification laws, or relocation of polling places. For many years after its passage, Section 5 was the workhorse of the VRA. In order to obtain preclearance, a covered jurisdiction would have to demonstrate that the change was made without a discriminatory purpose and that it would not make the affected minority groups worse off.

The expansion of voting rights ushered in a long-overdue wave of reforms: In 1971 the legal voting age was reduced from twenty-one to eighteen; in 1975 voting rights were expanded to protect non-English speakers; in 1982 Congress authorized voting protections for people with disabilities; in 1993 in order to attract more voters to the polls, Congress passed the National Voter Registration Act, better known as the "motor voter" law, which allowed citizens to register to vote when they applied for their drivers' licenses.[103] But for every step forward, pernicious attempts to frustrate Black voter turnout continued at the state and municipal levels. Between 1982 and 2006, DOJ objections blocked more than seven hundred changes to voting procedures based on a determination that the changes were discriminatory. Further, as the Supreme Court would later note, "Congress found that the majority of DOJ objections included findings of discriminatory intent, and that the changes blocked by preclearance were 'calculated decisions to keep minority voters from fully participating in the political process.'"[104]

A showdown was imminent, and it arrived in 2010, when Shelby County, Alabama, filed suit asking a federal court in Washington,

DC, to declare Section 5 of the Voting Rights Act unconstitutional. Then, in 2013, the Supreme Court struck a blow to the act. In *Shelby County v. Holder*, the Supreme Court, in a 5–4 opinion authored by Chief Justice John Roberts, effectively gutted Section 5's preclearance requirements, holding that the formula by which Congress determined which jurisdictions would be subject to these requirements was unconstitutional. Despite recognizing that "voting discrimination still exists," Chief Justice Roberts concluded that the VRA's coverage formula for preclearance—the "disparate treatment of the States"—was not sufficiently justified by congressional findings and, therefore, could not stand.[105] At bottom, the Court concluded that while the VRA's coverage formula may once have been justified by data showing discrimination in voter turnout and registration, improvement in those metrics since the act's passage meant that the formula was no longer warranted. In dissent, Justice Ruth Bader Ginsburg highlighted the puzzling nature of this rationale, noting that "throwing out preclearance when it has worked and is continuing to work to stop discriminatory changes is like throwing away your umbrella in a rainstorm because you are not getting wet."[106]

The fallout from *Shelby County* was swift: Within two hours after the Supreme Court issued its decision, the Texas attorney general tweeted that the state would immediately reinstitute its strict photo ID law, which had previously been struck down by a federal court under the VRA's preclearance procedures.[107] After that, the North Carolina General Assembly amended a pending bill to make its voter ID law stricter and added other provisions eliminating or restricting opportunities to vote that had been beneficial to minority voters.[108] In a report issued five years after the opinion, the U.S. Commission on Civil Rights outlined the passage of restrictive voter ID laws and other discriminatory voting practices in the wake of *Shelby County*, as well as the decrease in VRA enforcement actions by the Department of Justice.[109]

As a result of the decision in *Shelby County*, attention shifted to Section 2 of the VRA, which, as described above, provides a cause of action to challenge voting practices that reduce minority citizens' ability to vote. Adopted essentially as an enforcement mechanism for the Fifteenth Amendment's guarantee that the right to vote cannot be abridged "on account of race, color, or previous condition of servitude," Section 2 allows voters to seek judicial relief if they believe that a law "results in a denial or abridgement of the right of any citizen of the United States to vote on account of race." Section 2 is often described as adopting a "results test," because its plain language prohibits discriminatory results, not merely discriminatory intent.

Once again, however, the Supreme Court stepped in to undermine enforcement of the right to vote. In *Brnovich v. Democratic National Committee*, decided in 2021, the Court upheld two Arizona voting provisions that Democrats and civil rights groups challenged under Section 2 as disproportionately burdening minority voters.[110] In a 6–3 opinion authored by Justice Samuel Alito, the Court limited the VRA by suggesting a number of factors that should be considered when assessing whether a law violates Section 2—which, as Justice Elena Kagan's dissent pointed out, amounts to "a list of mostly made-up factors, at odds with Section 2 itself," all of which "cut in one direction—toward limiting liability for race-based voting inequalities."[111] The majority would seem to forgive some racially discriminatory burdens as inconsequential, and would ask only whether a discriminatory law *"reasonably pursue[s] important state interests."*[112] Though time will tell exactly how *Brnovich* might empower states to discriminate against minority voters, the decision was a major setback for voting rights advocates. And in "bypassing the Court's interpretive commitments from recent antidiscrimination cases, *Brnovich* foretells further hostility to the disparate impact theory of discrimination under other antidiscrimination statutes that are also critical to democracy."[113]

The fallout from *Shelby County v. Holder* continues to the present day. As FiveThirtyEight, an American website that focuses on opinion poll analysis, reported in 2021, "In the aftermath of the 2020 election, Republican lawmakers have pushed new voting restrictions in nearly every state. From making it harder to cast ballots early to increasing the frequency of voter roll purges, at least 25 new restrictive voting laws have been enacted, with more potentially on the horizon."[114]

IN CONTEMPORARY AMERICA, BLACK AMERICANS' TREATMENT WITHIN THE CRIMINAL JUSTICE SYSTEM REMAINS SEPARATE AND UNEQUAL

The historical incidence of discrimination against Black Americans within the criminal justice system is well documented, from the Black Codes to the routine denial of due process, lynchings, "convict leasing" (a post–Civil War government-revenue-generating scheme in which southern states leased quasi-enslaved unpaid prisoners to private business), false convictions, the contemporary crises of Black citizens' being twice as likely as white people to be killed by police,[115] to Black men and women being overrepresented in prisons, and Black men being overrepresented on death row.

Fortunately, in recent years these ongoing miscarriages of justice have attracted the increased, and urgent, attention they deserve. While the current focus on police shootings and Black overrepresentation in prisons is warranted, equal public scrutiny needs also to be directed at what, holistically, is a biased system that discriminates against Black citizens at every step along the criminal justice continuum: from profiling and pull-overs to arrests and prosecutions and to sentencing and incarceration.

For Black Americans, "separate and unequal" in the eyes of the law starts early: A 2018 study by the Campaign for Youth Justice, for example, showed that Black youths, who account for only 14 percent of the youth population, make up 53 percent of minors transferred to adult court for offenses.[116] From their teen years to adulthood, contentious interactions with the police are central components of the lived experience of millions of Black Americans. Black neighborhoods are subject to higher rates of police-initiated contact, regardless of actual local crime rates, resulting in over-policing of lower-level crime and behaviors. Yet research has shown that these same neighborhoods are underpoliced when calls for police support are issued by residents.[117]

On the subject of profiling during pull-overs, a large-scale national study of fifty-six policing agencies' practices that was published by the *Washington Post* in 2020 reported that between 2011 and 2018, 95 million traffic stops were made in the country. Black motorists were much more likely to be pulled over than white motorists, and be searched after a stop—although white drivers were *more* likely to be found with illicit drugs.[118] Washington, DC, offers a snapshot of the Black experience in our major cities: Over one four-week period in 2019, District police officers made eleven thousand stops. Black motorists accounted for 70 percent of them, despite being only 46 percent of the population.[119]

Small towns and quasi-rural communities are equally inhospitable to Black residents. For example, the seat of Albemarle County, Virginia, is the City of Charlottesville, where Black men comprise

8.5 percent of the population but more than 50 percent of the arrests. In the surrounding county, where Black citizens comprise a mere 4 percent of the population, they accounted for 38 percent of arrests.[120] And the arrests are frequently for misdemeanors. In 2018, for example, the *Boston University Law Review* reported that the "black arrest rate is at least twice as high as the white arrest rate for disorderly conduct, drug possession, simple assault, theft, vagrancy, and vandalism." Further, the report noted, "the black arrest rate for prostitution is almost five times higher than the white arrest rate, and the black arrest rate for gambling is almost ten times higher."[121] As the American Civil Liberties Union reports, Black Americans are incarcerated for drug offenses at a rate ten times greater than that of white Americans, despite the fact that Black people and white people use illegal drugs at roughly the same rates.[122]

Study after study has likewise confirmed bias in prosecutorial decision making. People of color are more likely to be prosecuted; they are likely to be charged under "habitual offender" statutes more often than white people; they are more likely to be detained pretrial because they lack resources to pay fines, fees, and bail; they are more likely to be denied bail altogether; and they are more likely than white people to be offered plea deals that include jail time.[123]

And the experience of Black Americans ensnared in the criminal justice web is also unequal once they stand before judges. As the U.S. Sentencing Commission found, Black defendants receive more severe sentences than their white counterparts.[124] As a *Washington Post* investigation revealed, "When black men and white men commit the same crime, black men on average receive a sentence almost 20 percent longer."[125]

In recent years, much attention has been focused on the Violent Crime Control and Law Enforcement Act of 1994, commonly referred to as the 1994 Crime Bill, which was signed into law by President Bill

Clinton and contained the now-infamous "three-strikes" provision, which called for mandatory life sentences for those who committed a violent felony and had two previous convictions. But to fully understand the explosion in the U.S. prison population, we need to look further back, to the early 1970s, when, after fifty years of stability, the rate of incarceration in the United States began a sustained period of growth. Between 1972 and 2007, the number of U.S. residents incarcerated in prisons and jails quintupled.[126] And it was Black Americans who were disproportionately sent to prison: By the twenty-first century, Black Americans were incarcerated in state prisons across the country at nearly five times the rate of white Americans[127] and were 3.5 times as likely to be incarcerated in local jails.[128] The impetus for the prison population explosion was the "War on Drugs," declared by President Richard Nixon, who during a 1971 press conference declared drug abuse "public enemy number one."[129] Shortly thereafter, the press popularized the term. The drug laws, as John Ehrlichman, who served as President Nixon's counsel and assistant to the president for domestic affairs between 1969 and 1973, admitted a generation later, were inherently political. In 1994 Ehrlichman told *Harper's* reporter Dan Baum that "the Nixon campaign in 1968, and the Nixon White House after that, had two enemies: the antiwar left and black people. You understand what I'm saying? We knew we couldn't make it illegal to be either against the war or blacks, but by getting the public to associate the hippies with marijuana and blacks with heroin, and then criminalizing both heavily, we could disrupt those communities. We could arrest their leaders, raid their homes, break up their meetings, and vilify them night after night on the evening news. Did we know we were lying about the drugs? Of course we did."[130]

A decade later, the Reagan administration continued the momentum. In his first term, President Reagan signed the Comprehensive Crime Control Act of 1984, which expanded penalties for possession of cannabis, established a federal system of mandatory minimum sentences, and established procedures for civil asset forfeiture.[131] According to historian Elizabeth Hinton, Reagan "led Congress in criminalizing drug users, especially African American drug users, by concentrating and stiffening penalties for the possession of the crystalline rock form of cocaine, known as 'crack,' rather than the crystallized methamphetamine that White House officials recognized was as much of a problem among low-income white Americans."[132] And support for the president's crusade, as Hinton noted in her book about the topic, *From the War on Poverty to the War on Crime: The Making of Mass Incarceration in America*, was bipartisan.[133]

Although crime rates in the United States declined steadily after 1991, the number of incarcerated Americans increased from approximately 350,000 in 1990 to more than 2 million in 2015. In absolute numbers, the country has the dubious distinction of jailing more of its residents than any nation in the world: 2.1 million people.[134] With less than 5 percent of the world's population, by 2015 the United States held nearly 25 percent of the world's prisoners. And the percentage of Black Americans in those prisons, 38 percent, is three times their proportion in the general population. White people, on the other hand, account for 76 percent of the general population but only 58 percent of the prison population.[135] Indeed, among Black men, one in three can expect to be incarcerated in his lifetime, compared to one in seventeen white men, according to a 2018 report issued by the Vera Institute of Justice. And Black women are similarly impacted: One in eighteen Black women born in 2001— and now in her early 20s—is likely to be incarcerated during her lifetime, compared to one in 111 white women.[136]

Once inside the walls of a prison, men of color are overrepresented in solitary confinement and may be perceived by officers as greater disciplinary and physical threats than the white inmate population.[137]

Finally, for inmates who have come to the literal, bitter end of the criminal justice journey—those on death row—the racial disparities are unsettlingly disproportionate. In 1980, 54 percent of death-row prisoners were white; by 2019, 58 percent were people of color.[138] Indeed, one of the starkest Black-white divisions within the criminal justice system is reflected in the number of persons executed in interracial murder cases: Since 1977, twenty-one white defendants have been executed for murdering a Black victim. The number of Black defendants executed for murdering a white victim: three hundred.[139] The American system of incarceration has been described as "the new Jim Crow."

Fortunately, after years of aggressive campaigning, civil and human rights groups are finally narrowing the incarceration gap. According to a recent Pew Research Center report, "At the end of 2017, federal and state prisons in the United States held about 475,900 inmates who were Black and 436,500 who were white—a difference of 39,400. Ten years earlier, there were 592,900 black and 499,800 white prisoners—a difference of 93,100."[140]

Brown, the civil rights movement, and affirmative action gave a large cohort of Americans permission to believe that America has delivered on its promise to level the playing field and deliver equal opportunity to its Black citizens. But events that transpired since 2010, including but not limited to the formation of Black Lives Matter in 2013 and the murder of George Floyd in 2020, revoked the permission some Americans granted themselves to avert their gaze from the legacy of racism in the country. And as white America currently confronts the most serious reckoning over race in three generations, the stakes are now higher than ever for Black citizens and affirmative action, as we will see in Chapter 4.

The Necessity of Both a Social and a Judicial Reckoning on Race

In the third decade of the twenty-first century, the debate over affirmative action remains contentious. The standoff continues between those who believe, as a matter of moral obligation, that the nation must do more to redress past wrongs and those who believe the nation has already remediated past wrongs and need do no more.

In higher education, on a practical level, the standoff continues between those who insist the college admissions process should, essentially, be limited to mathematical metrics (i.e., grades and test scores) and those who believe grades and test scores should be one of many factors in the admissions equation—along with leadership qualities, personal talents, race and ethnicity, family circumstances, *and* the admissions officer's judgment regarding which combination of students will yield both an optimized learning environment and, post-graduation, a better society.

And, as a matter of legal interpretation, disagreement continues between those who aspire to colorblindness and those who defend the need for color-consciousness.

Achieving consensus on affirmative action seems all the more unlikely when we consider that, since *Brown*, progress for America's

Black citizens has occurred, paradoxically, both rapidly and glacially. By almost any measure, the lived experience of Black Americans is undisputedly better today than under Jim Crow. Yet, as we discussed in Chapter 3, compared to white people—as well as Latinx, Asian Americans, and other minorities—Black citizens today live in what is essentially a resegregated, separate and unequal America, one bearing striking and unnerving resemblances to that in the period of *Brown*.

NON-RACE-BASED AFFIRMATIVE ACTION

Another affirmative action challenge facing admissions officers in higher education today is the changing makeup of the U.S. population. The racial and ethnic composition of the country has altered significantly over the course of the past seven decades. What was, literally, a black-and-white issue in 1954 (when 89 percent of the country was white and 10 percent was Black)[1] is now a "gray" issue, the result of massive demographic shifts since 1965. For it was in that year that Congress passed the Immigration and Nationality Act, also known as the Hart-Celler Act.[2] This law abolished the racially biased "National Origins Formula," which, since the 1920s, had ensured that policies governing immigration into the United States overwhelmingly favored white northwestern Europeans. The Hart-Celler Act removed de facto discrimination against southern and eastern Europeans and also opened America's doors to citizens from other continents. America also accommodated an increased number of political refugees from Soviet-controlled states, the Middle East and Africa, Latin America, and Southeast Asia.

Today, 62 percent of America is white, 18 percent Hispanic, 13 percent Black, and 6 percent Asian.[3] Accordingly, the current ethnic and racial composition of the nation's college campuses compared to the time of *Brown*—or even *Bakke*—is strikingly different. A quick perusal of the yearbooks of the co-authors' respective universities, Columbia and Chicago, offers a glimpse into these sweeping changes. The photos in the yearbooks from the 1950s are overwhelmingly white and predominantly male. Today's yearbooks, in addition to featuring white male faces, are filled with images of Black students, Asian students, Latinx students, LGBTQ+ students—and, significantly, more female students, who now actually outnumber males on American college and university campuses. Further, all things being essentially equal (grades, test scores, extracurricular activities, and so on,) how is an admissions officer to choose between a student born to, say, two wealthy Black parents and a half-Black, half-white student born into a low-income family, especially when the latter student is just as likely as the former to be viewed and treated by society as Black?

This has both admissions officers and applicants asking: *Who, exactly, qualifies as a "diversity candidate" in the 2020s?* And: *Are some diverse students in the 2020s somehow "more diverse" than others?*

Against this backdrop, affirmative action's critics contend that this increased demographic complexity justifies dismantling affirmative action altogether and that the way forward is to adopt a purely non-race-conscious, "meritocratic" admissions model and hope for the best or to achieve racial and ethnic diversity using other surrogate criteria (e.g., income status). But it is our strongly held view that *precisely because of this increased demographic complexity* we need affirmative action now more than ever, because Black students remain at the back of the line—which is getting even longer. Accordingly, we must ensure that Black students, in particular, are not excluded after having been shut out for centuries.

So, yes, we must protect and defend affirmative action. But rather than continue to debate (and litigate) the details of how the policy is applied, the central argument of this book is that the constitutional rationale *for the policy itself* needs to be reappraised—and changed. For the topic of this book is not, or not only, "diversity in education" and how that elevates the learning experience of all students but, more broadly, and far more important, it is about America's duty to correct the injustices that have been inflicted, uniquely, on Black Americans and inhibited their opportunity to develop and express their full talents, which are equal to those of any other group. While in education, specifically, over the past seven decades *Brown's* effort to create equal opportunity and remediate past injustice has driven progress for Black Americans, we contend that there is not nearly enough progress. And we believe that such remediation efforts must continue, potentially, for generations to come, because the damage done to Black Americans between 1619 and 1954—a 335-year span—has not been undone in 69 years. To that end, what we are asking of jurists, colleges and universities, and everyday Americans is to draw on their capacity for deep empathy and a clear-eyed understanding of reality, all of which was truly the beating heart of the *Brown* decision. We are asking for a determination to see clearly, to confront, and then to purposefully live by the principles of American justice. Because the rationale behind what a court (or a society) decides—the reason for it—is the most important matter to be resolved, especially at the outset. And, sadly, for too long, *Bakke* has incapacitated our ability to talk about this openly and honestly. Our aim, then, is to expand what has become a fairly narrow (and contentious) discussion about a policy into a broader discussion about principle.

While framing the appropriate constitutional rationale for affirmative action is the central goal of this volume, we would add our perspectives on the current debates about the policies themselves. We recognize that there are many critics who contend that affirmative action should be abandoned because it is either illegal, inefficacious, or both. While opposition to affirmative action is on most days expressed in legal and constitutional terms, affirmative action's opponents also criticize the policy on a parallel track, in a social and environmental context. Critics ask rhetorical questions designed to cast doubt on the efficacy of the policy. Often the questions either directly address or slyly allude to a notion of "belonging."

Among them are the following:

"Might it be possible that the beneficiaries of affirmative action are actually harmed more than helped by the policy, inasmuch as it may promote racial hostility against those who don't 'fit in'?"

"Might Black students, who, compared to their white counterparts, may appear to be less prepared to thrive in a rigorous academic environment, actually perform better and have an overall richer experience at a less competitive school?"

"Might Black students fare better in both school and in life if they attended a college or university they could get into without taking race into account?"

"Justice Powell, in Bakke, contended that 'the general benefits of diversity' would be accrued by all students—Black, white, Latinx, Asian, LGBTQ+, and so on. But step foot on a college campus today, and you'll notice that these various groups self-segregate: in clubs, at lunch tables, at events, in dormitories. Indeed, dozens of campuses nationwide, including several prestigious schools, now offer segregated residences, segregated orientation programs, and even segregated graduation ceremonies.[4] Doesn't this prove that being educated in a 'diverse' environment is no better than being educated in a non-or less-diverse environment?"

"Wouldn't it be better to achieve the same degree of racial and ethnic diversity by using other race-neutral criteria—such as family income or socioeconomic status—thereby avoiding the contentious issues about affirmative action altogether?"

Let us address these questions.

Decades' worth of social science research shows that increased diversity on campus results in much more satisfying experiences for *all* students.[5] But, more important, this is where the understanding of the legacy of discrimination is fundamental, not only in mandating affirmative action as a matter of justice but also in seeing how "diversity" works and how "merit" is a very complex matter.

One of America's leading scholars on race, Claude Steele, a social psychologist and emeritus professor at Stanford University, has written extensively on the subject of "stereotype threat," which occurs when people are or perceive themselves to be at risk of conforming to stereotypes about their social group. Stereotype threat creates an unvirtuous feedback loop, reinforcing stubbornly held attitudes one group has about another group.[6] And one way to eradicate the threat is to increase, not reduce, diversity within an institution.

In his book *Whistling Vivaldi*, Steele examined the findings of studies of the concept of "critical mass," defined as "the point at which there are enough minorities in a setting, like a school or a workplace, that individual minorities no longer feel uncomfortable there because they are minorities—in our terms, they no longer feel an interfering level of identity threat."[7] By way of example, Steele highlights a study by organizational psychologist Richard Hackman and his colleague Jutta Allmendinger that examined the concept of critical mass in relation to the incorporation of women into symphony orchestras. "In orchestras with a small percentage of women—in the 1 to 10 percent range, women . . . felt intense pressure to prove themselves and to fit a male model of what a good orchestra member is. Orchestras in which the percentage of women approached 20 percent or so—some degree of critical mass—still had problems, problems that were different from those when women were only tokens in the orchestra—greater gender fractiousness, for example—but problems nonetheless. It wasn't until the percentage of women in an orchestra reached about 40 percent that men and women alike began to report more satisfying experiences."[8]

The assertion that Black students would be happier or more successful in a less rigorous academic setting, the "mismatch argument," has also been discredited. Indeed, the research demonstrates that *all* students, regardless of race, demographics, or test scores, are more likely to graduate from the most selective schools that will admit them.[9]

Matthew Chingos, a senior fellow and director of the Education Policy Program at the Urban Institute, former Princeton University president William Bowen, and former president of Macalester College Michael McPherson highlighted this finding in their book *Crossing the Finish Line: Completing College at America's Public Universities.* The authors analyzed databases tracking students who enrolled in twenty-one flagship state universities in 1999, as well as a comparative database that tracked several statewide higher education systems. They used this information to compare Black men with high school grade-point averages below 3.0 who enrolled in the most selective flagships to those who enrolled in less selective flagships and those who enrolled in the least selective flagships. They concluded that increased rigor translated into higher graduation rates for this cohort of Black men: with a significantly higher percentage graduating from the most selective institutions than from mid-tier or the least selective institutions.[10]

Living and studying in a high-expectation environment, among high-achieving peers, delivers better outcomes and contradicts the notion that Black and other minority students would be better off in a less rigorous environment. The message for Black men (and other minority groups): Go to the best place that will admit you.[11] This research was cited in an amicus brief filed in support of the University of Texas, in *Fisher*:

> The stigma and mismatch arguments offered by Petitioner and her *amici curiae* ignore the wealth of data showing that minority students gain significant educational and economic benefits through their attendance at selective institutions—including higher graduation rates and increased earnings and labor force participation following graduation. . . . These findings underscore the Court's prior determination that "universities . . . represent the training ground for a large number of our Nation's leaders," as well as the importance of the University's ensuring that "the path to leadership be visibly open to talented and qualified individuals of every race and ethnicity."[12]

Further, to those who assert that affirmative action's efficacy is suspect because Black and white students (and other minority cohorts) may, on their arrival at the university, be prone to self-segregate, we believe the following: First, many Black students—as well as many white students—spent their K-12 years geographically segregated (which, as we have argued earlier, is significantly the legacy of discrimination). Thus, many encounter each other for the first time at university. Accordingly, it should neither surprise nor shock anyone that students may initially gravitate to others who look like them or have shared backgrounds and lived experiences. Second, we should not confuse the formation of various alliance groups on campus—the Black Students Organization, the Queer Alliance, the Latinx Professional Education Network, and so on—with resegregation. Do some like-minded students congregate in clubs or in dorms? Yes. Is their undergraduate experience socially, racially, and intellectually homogeneous? No. On our campuses, Columbia and Chicago, approximately six thousand diverse undergraduate students inhabit the same real estate, are educated in the same buildings, and sit shoulder-to-shoulder or collaborate in the same racially and ethically diverse classrooms. This exposure benefits all students—particularly white ones. Indeed, after Justice Powell formulated the "diversity rationale" in *Bakke,* social scientists set out to understand just how diverse learning environments shape educational experiences. We now know, as sociologist Mary Fischer of the University of Connecticut has reported, that campuses that are racially and ethnically diverse make students more likely to socialize with peers of other races;[13] they improve intellectual engagement and performance;[14] they bolster leadership skills;[15] they prompt increased civic engagement;[16] and they reduce prejudice in all students.[17]

Finally, it is demonstrably false that Black students fare better in both school and in life if they attended a college or university they could get into without taking race into account. A 2010 study by Deirdre Bowen, who is on the faculty of the Seattle University School of Law, compared students enrolled in universities with race-conscious admissions policies with students enrolled in universities in states that had barred race-conscious admissions.[18] Her research explored both the "internal stigma" experienced by minority students (e.g., feelings of doubt or inferiority) and "external stigma" caused when nonminority students questioned minority students' abilities and qualifications."[19] The percentage of minority students who experienced stigma was nearly 50 percent lower among students in schools with race-conscious admissions compared to those that barred race-conscious admissions.[20]

As we have noted, robust advocacy for and defense of race-conscious policies are unpopular in many quarters. Even strong supporters of affirmative action are wishing for surrogate criteria that will maintain the status quo but circumvent the debate, especially if the Court were to overrule *Grutter*. In any case, a new diversity metric has gained traction, a metric some hope may eventually supplant race as the principal lens through which diverse candidates are evaluated: social class. If admissions offices put more effort into admitting applicants with lower socioeconomic backgrounds, wouldn't that be good in itself *and* achieve racial and ethnic diversity? In principle, this compromise between race-consciousness and race-blindness sounds reasonable and fair. In practice, though, it is fraught with problems that portend results that work not on behalf of, but against, minority candidates.

If social and economic class were to become a key driver of admissions, white students would be advantaged because, simply stated, there are twice as many low-income white citizens as low-income Black citizens: Four in ten Americans living below the poverty line are white; Black Americans account for only two in ten.[21]

This fact was underscored in one of the amicus briefs filed in support of the University of Texas in *Fisher*:

> The consistent finding from a decade of studies is that race and socioeconomic status are simply not good substitutes for one another.[22] Many qualified African American and Latino college applicants are neither poor nor in the first generation of their family to go to college. Moreover, these groups represent only a small fraction of all low-income youth, and even a smaller fraction of high-achieving low-income youth.[23]

The most sophisticated analyses to date reinforce these conclusions. A 2015 study by Alon employs nuanced measures of class not previously considered (like family wealth) and relies not only on hypothetical scenarios, but on an assessment of a large scale class-based race-neutral admissions policy. Alon's study finds that "the student bodies of elite colleges would be substantially less diverse racially and ethnically under all types of class-based affirmative action relative to current race-based policy."[24] This conclusion holds even if most socioeconomically disadvantaged students apply to selective colleges.

Another rigorous 2015 study by Reardon and colleagues, who employ rich simulation techniques, finds that programs that consider only socioeconomic status, without considering race, fail to produce substantial racial diversity, even when socioeconomic status is given substantial weight in admissions.[25]

Next we will address the equally seductive appeal of an exclusively merit-based admissions formula.

EXCLUSIVELY "MERIT-BASED" ADMISSIONS

It is a fact that the university, for centuries, was the milieu of privileged white males. For the past several decades, though, great effort has been made to make universities more broadly representative of the society and more truly merit-based. And today, as a result, there is greater economic, gender, and racial diversity on campus. Historically marginalized groups have gained more visibility and voice. This is a welcome development.

But we now see that, in many respects, the old hierarchy has simply been replaced by a new one. As a result of four decades' worth of lawsuits over affirmative action policies in higher educa-tion, and the public attention those suits attracted, what was for decades an admissions process in highly selective schools has now been transformed into an admissions game as shrewd applicants (often steered by equally shrewd parents and "admissions coaches") have striven to present themselves as mirror images of the constit-uent elements that admissions officers are keen to see: from desired grade point averages and test scores to the "right" extracurricular activities, specific personal talents, racial background, socioeco-nomic circumstances, and so on. Indeed, the differences in overall qualifications these days are generally quite small. The applicants at highly selective schools are almost always in the 90th percentile (or even higher) of academic performers.

Black applicants, sadly, are disadvantaged in the contest, not because they lack comparable innate talent, but because, over the past several decades, the emergent meritocrats—often (though not always) with greater resources than Black Americans—have become extremely skilled at performing against the aforemen-tioned admissions metrics, a project that, in some cases, builds capacity across each category in a young person from as early as pre-kindergarten.

It is in this regard that the old inequalities perpetuated by one advantaged, entrenched group are being perpetuated by an emer-gent group of Americans who likewise enjoy structural advantages. If race was the natural advantage possessed by white male college students at the time of *Brown*, then high social class is emerging as the new advantage. Many of the members of the new meritocratic class that now comprises much of the student population at highly selective colleges and universities were raised in the so-called Super Zips—zip codes in the United States with the highest per capita income and college graduation rates. According to the *Washington*

Post, there are 650 such Super Zips, where a typical household earns over $120,000 a year, and 68 percent of the adults graduated from college.[26] Not surprisingly, the school systems in these communities—from Lexington, Massachusetts, to Fairfax County, Virginia, to Atherton, California—often are better funded, outperform the national average, or both.

While it is certainly true that some Black Americans live in Super Zips, the inhabitants of these communities are still predominantly white and possess two crucial advantages that many Black, Latinx, or low-income Americans who likewise aspire to the most competitive colleges do not: more time and more money. Time to shuttle children to private tutors, SAT prep classes, and summer enrichment camps—and the money to pay for them; time to shuttle children to years worth of private music lessons, debate competitions, or swim meets—and the money to pay for them; time to assist their children in the college application process—and the money required to apply to, on average, ten colleges or universities, about $50 to $75 per application.[27]

Let us now contrast the Super Zips with the nation's 1,036 majority-Black zip codes. Less than 2 percent of them can be defined as "prosperous"; seven in ten are considered "distressed."[28] In these zip codes, as in the Super Zips, parents dream of a quality education and upward mobility for their children, but the journey is far more harrowing. Single parents, many of them undereducated, are more prevalent in these communities. Incomes are lower. Crime is high. Unemployment is higher than in advantaged communities. Transportation is often an issue. Parents are more likely to have hourly jobs, and work evenings and weekends, than in the Super Zips, where, during Covid, millions of parents who work in "knowledge economy" jobs worked from home.

The meritocrats' college preparation project—a project laser-focused on gaining entry into a highly selective one—is often more difficult to execute in majority-Black communities because many families cannot pursue the enrichment projects available to residents of the Super Zips. Many cannot afford private music lessons, sports teams, and tutors, nor have they in many instances the time or transportation resources to shuttle their children to and fro. And most important, nor can they rely on their local public schools to deliver a comparable education. At the most basic level, students in such communities are not likely to receive quality instruction in their local school systems, which, on average, are among the worst performing in the nation. Private tutors are scarce. Public school music programs and athletic departments have been either abolished outright or gutted. Thus, under the new rules of the meritocratic game, Black students may be less likely to participate in extracurricular activities. As a result of centuries' worth of economic, educational, and social hardship, Black students are often competing at a major disadvantage.

As a result, across higher education, admissions officers are today far more aware of the limitations of meritocratic measures, in particular, standardized tests such as the ACT, SAT, GRE, and LSAT. Increasingly, the data tells us that these measures of merit are not in fact very good at measuring merit. The University of California at Berkeley's Center for Studies in Higher Education, a multidisciplinary research and policy center, has tracked millions of students over the course of decades and shown that SAT scores are not a good predictor of a student's first-year grades and are actually *worse* at predicting later outcomes.[29] Instead, four years' worth of consistently high marks in high school (which reflect not only intellectual talent but, equally important, work ethic and determination) are a more reliable predictor of success. Equally problematic is the fact that such tests have been shown to discriminate by race and income level. Scores on SATs correlate almost as much with one's income as they do with a second taking of the test. As Claude Steele notes, such tests "are too shaped by one's position in the racially stratified system of educational advantages and disadvantages. When they are used to inform admission decisions, they can wind up recapitulating the inequalities that are inherent in that system—laundering differences in advantage as differences in ability and promise."[30]

The children of low-income and minority families may have the same raw intellectual capabilities as their wealthy, privately educated peers, but the contexts in which they learn—in classrooms, during dinner table conversation, the media they consume—can differ widely. In short, social class, and the "caste" into which one is born in America, can profoundly affect, for example, a test-taker's degree of "cultural literacy," ability to understand literary allusions, gain exposure to esoteric STEM concepts, and so on. To that end, the Pulitzer Prize–winning journalist and author Isabel Wilkerson has written extensively about the phenomenon of caste, the rigid form of social stratification most often associated with Indian society, and how it is both ingrained and expressed, sometimes overtly, more often subtly, in American culture. Caste is characterized by the hereditary transmission of social rank, privileges and restrictions, occupations, and shared cultural features. America, Wilkerson argues, has since its founding, had a caste system akin to India's. And just as the "untouchable" Dalits of India are relegated to the lowest stratum of that nation, Black Americans have from the outset been relegated to the subordinate caste. In her book *Caste* Wilkerson makes an important distinction between caste and class, and sees them as separate measures of one's standing in society. Social class, Wilkerson asserts, is "marked by a level of education, income, and occupation as well as the attendant characteristics, such as accent, taste, and manners that flow from socioeconomic status. These can be acquired through hard work and ingenuity or lost through poor decisions or calamity. If you can act your way out of it, then it is class, not caste. Through the years, wealth and class may have insulated some [Black] people born into the subordinate caste in America but not protected them from humiliating attempts to put them in their place or remind them of their caste position."[31]

To be sure, these are hard words to take, and the analogy may seem too extreme. But the insights into what it can be like to live in a society with a legacy of discrimination are notable and even profound.

In the second half of the twentieth century, affirmative action sought to narrow the gap between white and Black citizens. Today we now have a widening gap between a cohort of Americans who exemplify diversity and a cohort that exemplifies the meritocracy, as we saw in California with Proposition 209. To state it bluntly, the meritocratic model stacks the deck in privileged candidates' favor and stacks the deck against everyone else, and it is widening the gap between Black and white college applicants. This is why, in our view, now more than ever we must not abandon the promise made by *Brown* to Black America; we must not renege on our obligation to narrow that gap, particularly, it seems, when a large swath of Americans, including perhaps a majority of current Supreme Court justices, appear ready to do so.

PENDING SUPREME COURT CASES

In 2022 the Supreme Court announced its intention to add two separate affirmative action cases to its calendar: *Students for Fair*

Admissions v. Harvard and *Students for Fair Admissions (SFFA) v. University of North Carolina at Chapel Hill.* The Court's decision to hear these cases represents a head-on collision between proponents of meritocracy and proponents of diversity and of recognizing our nation's legacy of discrimination.

Both petitions arose from long-running lawsuits filed by Students for Fair Admissions (SSFA), a nonprofit foundation started by conservative activist Edward Blum and designed to support litigation that challenges racial and ethnic classifications and preferences in state and federal courts.[32] Both lawsuits take aim at *Grutter.* And both challenge universities' use of affirmative action in admissions. The two cases implicate distinct legal issues.

The first case, filed against Harvard University, contends that the university's race-conscious admissions policy discriminates against Asian American applicants in violation of Title VI of the Civil Rights Act of 1964. The plaintiffs seek to ban Harvard and other colleges from considering—or even knowing—the race of its applicants.[33]

As a result of the litigation, Harvard (presumably with great reluctance) was compelled to reveal its admissions formula, which is described below:

> Harvard's admissions process begins with recruiting efforts, which aim to attract high-achieving applicants of varied socio-economic, geographic, and racial backgrounds. Harvard then evaluates applications using a rigorous multistep process. Every application is read by a "first reader," who assigns numeric scores in six areas: academic, extracurricular, athletic, school support, personal, and overall. Applicants are interviewed by alumni or admissions officers, who also assign scores in the academic, extracurricular, personal, and overall categories. Applications are then considered by regional subcommittees, which make

recommendations to the full admissions committee. If a majority of the committee votes to admit an applicant, the applicant is tentatively admitted. The full committee vote, however, typically results in "a pool of more than 2,000 tentative admits, more than can be admitted." The committee accordingly "conducts a 'lop process' to winnow down the pool." Throughout the process, admissions officers are periodically provided with "one-pagers," which report "demographic characteristics of Harvard's applicant pool and admitted class and compares them to the previous year." One-pagers contain information including the applicant pool's distribution by geographic region, race, gender, intended concentration, legacy status, and whether applicants applied for financial aid. Harvard uses this information to avoid dramatic year-to-year "drop-offs in admitted students with certain characteristics, including race, due to inadvertence or lack of care." It also uses the one pagers to "forecast yield rates"—i.e., "the percent of admitted applicants who accept an offer"—because applicants of certain demographic groups "accept offers of admission at higher rates."[34]

While the disclosure of its admissions formula reveals no great surprise, the twist in the Harvard litigation is that this case differs from "classic" affirmative cases because instead of pitting (historically advantaged) white applicants against (historically disadvantaged) Black and brown applicants in a contest for coveted seats at highly selective colleges and universities, *SFFA v. Harvard* pits Asian Americans, one historically disadvantaged group, against—in addition to white applicants—historically disadvantaged Black, Latinx, and Native American applicants.[35] In short, Asian applicants, once discriminated against on the basis of their race and eventually granted entry into highly selective colleges and universities as a result of diversity policies, appear to be discounting the contribution that other minority groups make to educational diversity and the value of selective universities in helping realize the promise of *Brown*.

A brief case history: In 2014, SFFA filed its suit against Harvard.[36] The organization represented a group of anonymous Asian American plaintiffs who had been rejected by Harvard.

A year later, the Lawyers' Committee for Civil Rights Under Law, a nonprofit focused on securing equal justice for all under the law—in particular African Americans and other racial and ethnic minorities—intervened on behalf of current and prospective under-represented minority students at Harvard and submitted an amici brief in support of Harvard's motion to dismiss.[37] Asian Americans Advancing Justice, also keen to defend race-conscious admissions policies, joined this effort and filed briefs in support of Harvard.

In the autumn of 2018 the case arrived in the United States District Court for the District of Massachusetts. A year later, in October 2019, United States District Judge Allison Dale Burroughs ruled that Harvard College's admissions policies did not unduly discriminate against Asian Americans.

In February 2020 SFFA filed an appeal in the United States Court of Appeals for the First Circuit. It lost its case for the second time.

In both the initial hearing and the appeal, the Trump administration's Justice Department filed a friend-of-the-court brief, arguing that Harvard University unlawfully discriminated against Asian Americans. By singling out students according to race during the admissions process, the Justice Department contended, Harvard imposed "a racial penalty" on Asian American applicants.[38]

In late February 2021, nearly seven years after the proceedings were commenced and one month into a new presidential administration, SFFA petitioned the Supreme Court to hear the case. Three months later, Harvard filed its opposing brief seeking to have SFFA's petition rejected by the Supreme Court.

In orders issued in the summer of 2021, the Court requested that the U.S. government file a brief on its stance on the case. In the late autumn of 2021, the Biden administration's new solicitor general of the United States, Elizabeth Prelogar, filed a brief that defended Harvard's admissions policies; she urged the high court not to grant certiorari. We quote her rationale below:

> Revisiting this Court's settled precedent in the specific context of Harvard's admissions process would place the disruption of those reliance interests in stark relief. Harvard's approach has been a point of reference in decisions addressing other institutions' policies since *Bakke*. There, Justice Powell cited Harvard's process as "[a]n illuminating example" of how a school's compelling interest in student-body diversity can be pursued without quotas or racial balancing. The Court in *Grutter* likewise found a comparison to "Harvard's flexible use of race as a 'plus' factor" to be "instructive" and upheld the University of Michigan Law School's admissions policy because it resembled "the Harvard plan" in relevant respects. Conversely, *Gratz* held invalid Michigan's undergraduate admissions policy based in part on dissimilarities between it and Harvard's approach. Those decisions have invited colleges and universities to rely on the permissibility of a holistic, flexible approach like Harvard's as a benchmark in structuring their own admissions policies. It would profoundly unsettle expectations to declare retroactively that such reliance subjects those institutions to Title VI liability."[39]

The second case, filed by SFFA against the University of North Carolina at Chapel Hill, the state's flagship public university, argues that the university's consideration of race in its undergraduate admissions process violates both the Constitution and Title VI of Civil Rights Act of 1964, which was enacted to prevent recipients of federal funds from discriminating on the basis of race, color, or national origin, lest they lose federal funding.

A brief case history: In 2014 SFFA brought a lawsuit alleging that UNC Chapel Hill's undergraduate admissions policy violates the Fourteenth Amendment and Title VI because: (1) it does "not merely use race as a 'plus' factor in admissions decisions . . . to achieve student body diversity"; (2) there are available "race-neutral alternatives capable of achieving student body diversity"; and (3) using race as a factor in admissions at all is unconstitutional.[40]

After a federal district court in North Carolina rejected SFFA's arguments, the organization went directly to the Supreme Court, petitioning the justices to hear their case *before* the U.S. Court of Appeals for the Fourth Circuit could rule.

Notably, unlike the Harvard litigation, the UNC case does not contend that UNC discriminates against one specific minority group (i.e., Asian Americans). Instead, the plaintiffs allege that UNC impermissibly favors Black and Hispanic students over others (including Asian American and white students). Further, unlike Harvard, UNC is a public university and is therefore covered by the Fourteenth Amendment's guarantee of equal protection. So, whereas the legal claim in the Harvard case focuses on Title VI, the UNC petition squarely raises the question of whether affirmative action is constitutional. Further, as noted above, the case also differs in procedural terms: The Supreme Court took the rare step of agreeing to hear the case before the Fourth Circuit could rule on it, signaling that the Court is eager to decide the constitutional question presented in *SFFA v. University of North Carolina at Chapel Hill.*

Much is at stake.

The enjoined Harvard and UNC cases will be the first affirmative action cases to come before a Supreme Court whose composition has changed markedly since 2016's *Fisher II,* which was decided by a 4–3 vote (Justice Kagan recused herself from the case owing to her prior involvement as Solicitor General[41] and the ninth seat on the Court was vacant owing to the death of Justice Scalia).

Beginning in 2017, President Donald Trump's appointees have significantly reshaped the Court: Justice Gorsuch replaced Scalia, Justice Kavanaugh replaced Justice Kennedy, author of the *Fisher* opinion, and Justice Barrett replaced Justice Ginsburg, who had always been a strong supporter of affirmative action. During his confirmation process, legal experts expressed concern about Justice Kavanaugh's prior comments and rulings on equal protection issues related to affirmative action,[42] and the confirmation of Justice Barrett, many speculated, would portend a "colorblind" interpretation of the Equal Protection Clause among the conservative majority. Accordingly, there is now concern that these shifts would tilt the Court 6–3 against the constitutionality of affirmative action.

From the abolition of slavery to the Reconstruction era, through Jim Crow, *Brown* and the civil rights era, to the present, as affirmative action policies now confront an existential threat, we are reminded that Black Americans' quest for racial justice and equality has never proceeded "in a straight line of greater and greater freedom and greater and greater rights," as historian Eric Foner observes. Instead, he continues, "it's a much more complicated story of ups and downs, of rights gained and rights lost that have to be fought for another day." Accordingly, the same Supreme Court that got it so wrong so many times, especially during the Reconstruction era, now has a once-in-a-generation opportunity to protect and advance the ideals we claim most to value as Americans.[43]

LOOKING TO THE FUTURE: MARSHALL WAS RIGHT AND POWELL WAS WRONG

While we will resist the temptation to issue predictions about how the Court will rule in these two cases, it is probable, bordering on inevitable, that over the course of the next decade the contours of Black Americans' higher education journey—either forward or backward—will be shaped by this decision.

About one thing we are certain: Affirmative action is at a crossroads. On one hand, we cannot pretend it is 1954 anymore; on the other, in many ways America is still too much like it was in 1954. The repugnant white resistance to *Brown* and the civil rights movement, so prevalent in the 1950s and 1960s, faded into the background in American life in subsequent decades, or so we thought, until it resurfaced, most notably during 2017's "Unite the Right" rally in Charlottesville, Virginia. No reasonable person can deny the progress Black Americans have made, yet we dare not pretend that we are living in the colorblind America envisioned by Justice Sandra Day O'Connor two decades ago.

Six decades into the affirmative action project, proponents of the policy must, from both a legal and public discourse perspective, reclaim and reframe the debate.

First, we must reassert the original intent of affirmative action: to create opportunity for historically oppressed groups in general and Black Americans in particular, because the inhumanity inflicted on them in the form of chattel slavery and the social, economic, political, and professional disenfranchisement they experienced vis-à-vis other minority groups, was—and remains—unparalleled. At the same time, we must acknowledge that progress has been made, demographics have changed, and affirmative action is not and has never claimed to be a perfect solution to centuries' worth of discrimination against Black Americans.

Until or unless the courts reappraise the constitutional rationale for the policy itself, affirmative action, despite its imperfections, remains a critically important way to address discrimination in America against Black Americans. And, as America's current reckoning over race demonstrates, the need for affirmative action remains strong. It is higher education, perhaps more than any other American endeavor, that is uniquely ready to receive, prepare, and credential Black Americans for entry into and long-term success within America's, and the world's, leading institutions. And rather than accept an ever more diluted form of affirmative action in the years ahead, we have an obligation to redouble our efforts if we as a nation are serious about undoing the systemic racism that *Brown*, the civil rights movement, and a half century's worth of public policy initiatives hoped to ameliorate. Rather than sheepishly apologize for the necessity of affirmative action, then, we contend that its proponents should continue to champion it as an essential tool to deliver justice to Black Americans.

Accordingly, now is the time for leaders in higher education and elsewhere to protect, defend, and advocate for affirmative action, in courtrooms and in the court of public opinion. Affirmative action's proponents, especially those in higher education, have enjoyed qualified victories in the courts, but we need to do a better job now in persuading skeptics of its legitimacy and its importance.

While it is evident that a cohort of affirmative action's opponents at the extreme end of the spectrum are unreconstructed racists (whom we have no illusion will be persuaded to reverse their noxious views based on the arguments in this book or on the op-ed pages of newspapers and elsewhere), opportunity exists to remind skeptics of the policy at the opposite end of the spectrum that much work remains to be done to remedy past and present injustice.

To this cohort—which includes well-educated, high-achieving inhabitants of Super Zips, Asian Americans who aspire to Harvard, employees worried they will be passed over in favor of a "diversity candidate," and the current Chief Justice of the United States Supreme Court—we make this plea: If you truly want to see Black Americans ascend, we urge you to truly *see* Black Americans, to take a sober, clear-eyed look at their experience since *Brown* and honestly try to convince yourself and others that they play on a level playing field.

In 2014, seven years after Chief Justice Roberts, in *Parents Involved in Community Schools v. Seattle School District No. 1*, said, "The way to stop discrimination on the basis of race is to stop discriminating on the basis of race," Justice Sonia Sotomayor, in her dissenting opinion in another affirmative action case before the Court, *Schuette v. Coalition to Defend Affirmative Action*, said:

The way to stop discrimination on the basis of race is to speak openly and candidly on the subject of race . . . and to apply the Constitution with eyes open to the unfortunate effects of centuries of racial discrimination. . . . Race matters. Race matters in part because of the long history of racial minorities being denied access to the political process. . . . Race also matters because of persistent racial inequality in society—inequality that cannot be ignored and that has produced stark socioeconomic disparities. . . . And race matters for reasons that really are only skin deep, that cannot be discussed any other way, and that cannot be wished away. Race matters to a young man's view of society when he spends his teenage years watching others tense up as he passes, no matter the neighborhood where he grew up. Race matters to a young woman's sense of self when she states her hometown, and then is pressed, "No, where are you really from?," regardless of how many generations her family has been in the country. Race matters . . . because of the slights, the snickers, the silent judgments that reinforce that most crippling of thoughts: "I do not belong here."[44]

Second, campus admissions policies must continue to evolve. There are always a host of perplexing questions to be decided. For example, it is no secret among admissions officers that standardized tests such as the SAT and ACT favor upper-income candidates emerging from private schools or superior public schools. Should colleges and universities eliminate such tests altogether, in hopes of improving equity among applicants and diversity? Or should colleges and universities consider new pathways into highly selective schools that might have been unthinkable a generation ago, such as admitting community college transfer students (who are traditionally from lower-income families and often are minorities) who meet academic performance thresholds? This is an experiment currently under way at some, though not all, of the schools in the University of California system.[45] Further, how are admissions officers to make determinations about applicants who refuse to disclose their race? Or applicants who make difficult-to-verify "stretch claims" of personal hardship or membership in certain historically disadvantaged groups?

It would also be helpful for schools to dispel the myth that *every* graduate of a highly selective college or university will demonstrate unrivaled academic brilliance. Not all graduates of such institutions ascend to the Supreme Court, win Nobel Prizes, or become Fortune

500 CEOs. The fact is, at every college or university academic talent sorts itself out as one student will rank first in his or her class, and someone else will, invariably, rank last. Everyone else will land somewhere in between. This has been happening since Harvard College opened its doors in 1636.

For decades—centuries—competent, but hardly brilliant, white men attended our schools and attained nothing more than a "Gentleman's C." We are unaware of historical efforts to describe this phenomenon as "an erosion of standards." We are also confident in our assertion that many students of leading academic institutions have supplemented their education with tutoring or mentoring in order to overcome various academic struggles and earn a diploma.

At the same time, we should recognize that American higher education has for decades considered many characteristics in composing their student bodies, factors such as geography (national and international) and demonstrations of civic responsibility, all with an admirable and laudable objective of helping build a better nation. Other factors, such as legacy status, have far less social purpose and yet have been vigorously embraced by most selective colleges and universities. All this adds to the general point that we should embrace affirmative action with pride and purpose and not drift toward policies that will effectively exclude Black students. Instead, we need to increase success rates and, given that many of our Black students may be in the first or second generation of their family to attend university, may come from an economically disadvantaged family or community, or likely attended substandard public schools, it is our opinion that critics have put the question backward. Rather than ask, "Why should the university offer such students added support?" we contend the question should be "Why *wouldn't* the university offer such students added support?"

Finally, we would add, while stratospheric test scores and class rankings correlate highly with professional success after graduation, the inverse does not apply: Students who occupy the middle or lower ranks of top schools are not doomed to social or professional failure. Indeed, the overwhelming majority can and do make meaningful contributions to their chosen professions and to society.

Which now brings us to the Supreme Court. From a legal standpoint, we can and must allow the Fourteenth Amendment, which provides for equal protection under the law, to continue to protect and advance the interests of all Americans, especially minorities—now more than ever. Accomplishing this objective will require jurists, policymakers, opinion leaders, and media outlets to drive progress on two parallel tracks: to prevent discrimination and to promote equality. As a society, we have been far more successful at the former than the latter. Accordingly, in addition to evaluating the *content* of case law, we should more thoughtfully evaluate the *context*—past, present, and future—in which courts issue race-related rulings. That is why it is so perilous for the Court to decree that any policy aimed at increasing integration—in education, in housing, in people's economic lives—is unconstitutional.

The time has come for jurists to liberate affirmative action from the straitjacket imposed by Justice Powell in *Bakke*, when he recast a policy designed to secure equal opportunity and integration for Black Americans as one providing (mostly white) Americans with "the educational benefits of diversity." This was a compromise—and not a brave one. It was a standing down, a retreat from the promise articulated by *Brown*, as argued by Justice Marshall and accepted by Chief Justice Warren. Justice Powell may have wanted to move on from the legacies of segregation, but his diversity rationale in *Bakke* is simply not sufficient. Instead, we must be able to use affirmative action as a remedy to address the ongoing realities and consequences of racism in America, to help the country move forward and continue the progress we've made.

For these reasons, affirmative action cannot and must not be abandoned until it can be demonstrated that America has become a truly colorblind society; until it can be demonstrated that America no longer discriminates against its Black citizens; until it can be demonstrated that Black Americans have been fully integrated into American society; until it can be demonstrated that Black Americans enjoy equal access to the American Dream.

This is why we contend that those who believe affirmative action creates more problems than it corrects, or is a solution to a problem that is no longer a problem, are deeply misguided.

As students in the 1960s, we agreed wholeheartedly with Martin Luther King Jr. that our fellow countrymen and women should be judged by the content of their character—not the color of their skin. We still do. We were invested, as he was, in the notion of a colorblind society. In principle, this is a noble idea. But decades on, in practice, millions of Black Americans continue to be judged and disadvantaged as a result of the color of their skin.

Which brings us back to the key argument of this book: We need to face up to this reality, permit our institutions of higher learning to take steps to address it, and continue on the seminal path chartered by the Court in *Brown.*

NOTES

Acknowledgments

1. See Joseph Berger, "The Man Behind the V.," *New York Times*, April 13, 2003, https://www.nytimes.com/2003/04/13/education/the-man-behind-the-v.html.
2. See Jane Dailey, *Building the American Republic*, vol. 2, *A Narrative History from 1877* (Chicago: University of Chicago Press, 2018).

Introduction

1. "Executive Orders Disposition Tables," U.S. National Archives and Records Administration, updated August 15, 2016, https://www.archives.gov/federal-register/executive-orders/1961-kennedy.html.
2. "A Brief History of Affirmative Action," University of California at Irvine, accessed May 17, 2022, http://www.oeod.uci.edu/policies/aa_history.php.
3. U.S. Const. amend. XIV.
4. *Regents of the Univ. of Cal. v. Bakke*, 438 U.S. 265, 274 (1978).
5. *Slaughterhouse Cases*, 83 U.S. 36 (1872).
6. Jane Dailey, *Building the American Republic*, vol. 2, *A Narrative History from 1877* (Chicago: University of Chicago Press, 2018), 31.
7. *Civil Rights Cases*, 109 U.S. 3 (1883).
8. Ibid.
9. Ibid., 32.

10. Ibid., 33; *Williams v. Mississippi*, 170 U.S. 213 (1898).

11. *Plessy v. Ferguson*, 163 U.S. 537 (1896).

12. *Brown v. Board of Education of Topeka*, 347 U.S. 483 (1954).

13. *Loving v. Virginia*, 388 U.S. 1 (1967).

14. *New York Times Co. v. Sullivan*, 376 U.S. 254 (1964).

15. *Swann v. Charlotte-Mecklenburg Bd. of Educ.*, 402 U.S. 1 (1971).

16. *Regents of Univ. of California v. Bakke*, 438 U.S. 265 (1978).

17. Dailey, *Building the American Republic*.

18. *Grutter v. Bollinger*, 539 U.S. 306 (2003).

19. Ibid.

20. *Gratz v. Bollinger*, 539 U.S. 244 (2003).

21. *Fisher v. University of Texas*, 570 U.S. 297 (2013).

22. *Fisher v. University of Texas at Austin*, 579 U.S. 365 (2016).

23. Lee C. Bollinger, "Sixty Years Later, We Need a New *Brown*," *New Yorker*, May 16, 2014, https://www.newyorker.com/news/news-desk/sixty-years-later-we-need-a-new-brown.

24. Michael Gee, "Why Aren't Black Employees Getting More White-Collar Jobs?," *Harvard Business Review*, February 28, 2018, hbr.org/2018/02/why-arent-black-employees-getting-more-white-collar-jobs; *BOP Statistics: Inmate Race*, www.bop.gov/about/statistics/statistics_inmate_race.jsp.

25. Dailey, *Building the American Republic*, 232.

26. *Students for Fair Admissions, Inc. v. President and Fellows of Harvard College*, No. 15-1823 (1st Cir. 2015).

27. *Students for Fair Admissions, Inc. v. University of North Carolina*, et al., No. 1:2014cv00954—Document 79 (M.D.N.C. 2017).

28. *Regents of the Univ. of Cal. v. Bakke*, 438 U.S. 265, 274 (1978) (Marshall, T. dissenting).

Chapter 1

1. *2020 Profile of Older Americans*, Administration for Community Living, May 2021, https://acl.gov/sites/default/files/Aging%20and%20Disability%20in%20America/2020ProfileOlderAmericans.Final_.pdf.

2. Jane Dailey, *Building the American Republic*, vol. 2, *A Narrative History from 1877* (Chicago: University of Chicago Press, 2018).

3. Eric Foner, author of *Reconstruction: America's Unfinished Journey*, in a talk to the Century Association, February 2018 (YouTube: https://www.youtube.com/watch?v=49McwjkZmlw).

4. *Encyclopedia Britannica*, s.v. "Black Code," by the Editors of Encyclopedia Britannica, updated August 20, 2019, https://www.britannica.com/topic/black-code.

5. Dailey, *Building the American Republic*, 32.
6. Ibid., 35.
7. Ibid., 35–36.
8. *Plessy v. Ferguson*, 163 U.S. 537 (1896).
9. "Plessy v. Ferguson (1896)," National Archives, updated February 8, 2022, https://www.archives.gov/milestone-documents/plessy-v-ferguson.
10. Foner, talk to the Century Association.
11. Dailey, *Building the American Republic*, 82.
12. "The Great Migration (1910–1970)," National Archives, updated June 28, 2021, https://www.archives.gov/research/african-americans/migrations/great-migration.
13. Dailey, *Building the American Republic*, 98.
14. Ibid., 168, 171.
15. "FDR and the Four Freedoms Speech," Franklin D. Roosevelt Presidential Library and Museum, accessed October 3, 2022, https://www.fdrlibrary.org/four-freedoms.
16. Dailey, *Building the American Republic*, 183.
17. *Smith v. Allwright*, 321 U.S. 649 (1944).
18. Dailey, *Building the American Republic*, 197.
19. Risa L. Goluboff, *The Human Tradition in American Labor History*, ed. Aric Arnesen (Lanham, MD: Rowan and Littlefield, 2003).
20. U.S. Library of Congress, Congressional Research Service, *A Chronology of Housing Legislation and Selected Executive Actions, 1892–2003* (Washington: U.S. Government Printing Office, 2004).
21. Kevin Fox Gotham, "Racialization and the State: The Housing Act of 1934 and the Creation of the Federal Housing Administration," *Sociological Perspectives* 43, no. 2 (Summer 2000): 291–317, https://www.jstor.org/stable/1389798.
22. Larry Adelman, "Race: The Power of an Illusion," PBS, produced by California Newsreel, accessed June 2, 2022, https://www.pbs.org/race/000_About/002_06_a-godeeper.htm.
23. Ira Katznelson, *When Affirmative Action Was White: An Untold History of Racial Inequality in Twentieth-Century America* (New York: W. W. Norton, 2006).
24. Dailey, *Building the American Republic*, 211.
25. Ibid., 211–212.
26. U.S. House of Representatives, History, Art & Archives, "Black-American Members by Congress," accessed May 18, 2022, https://history.house.gov/Exhibitions-and-Publications/BAIC/Historical-Data/Black-American-Representatives-and-Senators-by-Congress/.
27. Dailey, *Building the American Republic*, 214.
28. Erick Johnson, "America's First Black Mayor, 50 Years Later," *Philadelphia Tribune*, November 17, 2017, https://www.phillytrib.com/news/across_

america/america-s-first-black-mayor-50-years-later/article_bac484d0-1dc3-54af-8017-719d77561daa.html.

29. Stanley Greenberg, *Race and State in Capitalist Development* (New Haven: Yale University Press, 1980), 231–233.

30. Abigail Thernstrom and Stephan Thernstrom, "Black Progress: How Far We've Come, and How Far We Have to Go," *Brookings*, March 1, 1998, https://www.brookings.edu/articles/black-progress-how-far-weve-come-and-how-far-we-have-to-go.

31. Jean Folger, "The History of Lending Discrimination," *Investopedia*, updated May 1, 2022, https://www.investopedia.com/the-history-of-lending-discrimination-5076948.

32. Mary S. Bedell, "Employment and Income of Negro Workers, 1940–1952," *Monthly Labor Review* (June 1953): 600, https://www.bls.gov/opub/mlr/1953/article/pdf/employment-and-income-of-negro-workers-1940-52.pdf.

33. Langston Hughes, *Selected Poems of Langston Hughes* (New York: Vintage, re-issue ed., 1990),,, 285.

34. Dailey, *Building the American Republic*, 231.

35. Ibid., 231–232.

36. *Brown v. Board of Education of Topeka*, 347 U.S. 483 (1954).

37. Dailey, *Building the American Republic*,232.

38. *McCabe v. Atchison, T. & S.F. Ry. Co.*, 235 U.S. 151 (1914).

39. *Buchanan v. Warley*, 245 U.S. 60 (1917).

40. *Missouri ex rel. Gaines v. Canada*, 305 U.S. 337 (1938).

41. *Sweatt v. Painter*, 339 U.S. 629 (1950).

42. *McLaurin v. Oklahoma State Regents*, 339 U.S. 637 (1950).

43. Bailey, *Building the American Republic*, 232.

44. Ibid., 231–232.

45. *Brown*, 347 U.S. at 493.

46. *Brown*, 347 U.S. at 494–495.

47. Dailey, *Building the American Republic*, 233.

48. Ibid., 234.

49. Ibid., 233–234.

50. Ibid., 234.

51. Ibid., 239.

52. Ibid., 238–239.

53. Charles J. Ogletree Jr., *All Deliberate Speed: Reflections on the First Half-Century of* Brown vs. Board of Education (New York: W. W. Norton, 2004), 10.

54. Trina Jones, "Brown II: A Case of Missed Opportunity," *Minnesota Journal of Law & Inequality* 24, no. 1 (2006), https://scholarship.law.umn.edu/cgi/viewcontent.cgi?article=1072&context=lawineq

55. Dailey, *Building the American Republic*, 253.

56. Ibid.

57. Ibid., 254.

58. Ibid.

59. "'Segregation Forever': A Fiery Pledge Forgiven, But Not Forgotten" (All Things Considered, NPR, January 10, 2013), https://www.npr.org/2013/01/14/169080969/segregation-forever-a-fiery-pledge-forgiven-but-not-forgotten.

60. Dailey, *Building the American Republic*, 259.

61. Kevin K. Gaines, *The End of the Second Reconstruction, Modern American History* 1 (2018): 113–119, https://www.cambridge.org/core/journals/modern-american-history/article/end-of-the-second-reconstruction/ECA03143E08ED9AFE85E0446B445E067.

62. Dailey, *Building the American Republic*, 256.

63. Ibid.

64. *Nat'l Ass'n for Advancement of Colored People v. State of Ala. ex rel. Patterson*, 357 U.S. 449 (1958).

65. *Bates v. City of Little Rock*, 361 U.S. 516, 523 (1960).

66. *Gibson v. Fla. Legislative Investigation Comm.*, 372 U.S. 539 (1963).

67. *Garner v. Louisiana*, 368 U.S. 157 (1961).

68. *Edwards v. South Carolina*, 372 U.S. 229 (1963).

69. *Cox v. Louisiana*, 379 U.S. 536 (1965).

70. *Brown v. Louisiana*, 383 U.S. 131 (1966).

71. *Gregory v. City of Chicago*, 394 U.S. 111 (1969); *Shuttlesworth v. Birmingham*, 394 U.S. 147 (1969).

72. *Nat'l Ass'n for Advancement of Colored People v. Button*, 371 U.S. 415 (1963); *First Amendment Encyclopedia*, s.v. "NAACP v. Button," by Sekou Franklin, 2009, https://www.mtsu.edu/first-amendment/article/69/naacp-v-button.

73. "Heed Their Rising Voices," National Archives, March 29, 1960, https://www.archives.gov/exhibits/documented-rights/exhibit/section4/detail/heed-rising-voices-transcript.html.

74. *New York Times Co. v. Sullivan*, 376 U.S. 254 (1964), at 367.

75. *First Amendment Encyclopedia*, s.v. "New York Times Co. v. Sullivan (1964)," by Stephen Wermiel, 2009, https://www.mtsu.edu/first-amendment/article/186/new-york-times-co-v-sullivan.

76. Dailey, *Building the American Republic*, 264.

77. Ibid., 265.

78. *Encyclopedia Britannica*, s.v. "Great Society," by the Editors of Encyclopedia Britannica, accessed October 3, 2022, https://www.britannica.com/event/Great-Society.

79. The Lyndon Baines Johnson Presidential Library, Commencement Speech at Howard University, 6/4/65. MP2265–66, YouTube (May 31, 2013), https://www.youtube.com/watch?v=vcfAuodA2x8.

80. Dailey, *Building the American Republic*, 265.

81. *Martin Luther King, Jr. Encyclopedia,* s.v. "Poor People's Campaign," the Martin Luther King, Jr. Research and Education Institute, accessed May 19, 2022, https://kinginstitute.stanford.edu/encyclopedia/poor-peoples-campaign.

82. *Martin Luther King, Jr. Encyclopedia,* s.v. "March on Washington for Jobs and Freedom," the Martin Luther King, Jr. Research and Education Institute, accessed May 19, 2022, https://kinginstitute.stanford.edu/encyclopedia/march-washington-jobs-and-freedom.

83. *Encyclopedia Britannica,* s.v. "Poor People's March," by the Editors of Encyclopedia Britannica, accessed May 19, 2022, https://www.britannica.com/topic/Poor-Peoples-March.

84. Kate McLaughlin, "Eight Unforgettable Ways 1968 Made History," CNN, July 31, 2014, https://www.cnn.com/2014/07/31/us/1968-important-events/index.html.

85. Adam Clymer, "Strom Thurmond, Senate Institution Who Fought Integration, Dies at 100," *New York Times,* June 28, 2003, https://www.nytimes.com/2003/06/28/us/strom-thurmond-senate-institution-who-fought-integration-dies-at-100.html.

86. Stephen Smith and Katie Ellis, "Campaign '68: Part 3," *APM Reports,* October 2018, https://features.apmreports.org/arw/campaign68/b3.html.

87. Kit R. Roane and B. Drummond Ayres Jr., "The Battle for Busing," *Retro Report,* September 9, 2013, https://www.retroreport.org/transcript/the-battle-for-busing.

88. *Alexander v. Holmes County Bd. of Ed.,* 396 U.S. 19 (1969); Dailey, *Building the American Republic,* 296.

89. P. R. Lockhart, "Joe Biden's Record on School Desegregation Busing, Explained," *Vox,* updated July 16, 2019, https://www.vox.com/policy-and-politics/2019/6/28/18965923/joe-biden-school-desegregation-busing-democratic-primary.

90. The Economist Data Team, "Segregation in America," *Economist,* updated January 4, 2020, https://www.economist.com/graphic-detail/2018/04/04/segregation-in-america.

91. Ritu Prasad, "Kamala Harris–Joe Biden Row: What Is Desegregation Busing?," *BBC News,* June 28, 2019, https://www.bbc.com/news/world-us-canada-48803864.

92. *Swann v. Charlotte-Mecklenburg Bd. of Educ.,* 402 U.S. 1 (1971); Dailey, *Building the American Republic,* 296.

93. Richard Nixon Foundation, "Nixon, the Supreme Court, and Busing," April 12, 2015, https://www.nixonfoundation.org/2015/04/nixon-the-supreme-court-and-busing/

94. Dailey, *Building the American Republic,* 297.

95. Roane and Ayres, "Battle for Busing," 99.

96. Education: Coleman: Some Second Thoughts, *Time*, September 15, 1975, https://content.time.com/time/subscriber/article/0,33009,917827-1,00.html.

97. Domenico Montanaro, "Listen: Biden Supported a Constitutional Amendment to End Mandated Busing in 1975," *NPR*, July 28, 2019, https://www.npr.org/2019/06/28/736995314/listen-biden-supported-a-constitutional-amendment-to-end-mandated-busing-in-1975; Derrick Bryson Taylor, Sheryl Gay Stolberg, and Astead W. Herndon, "A Brief History of Joe Biden and School Busing," *New York Times*, July 15, 2019, https://www.nytimes.com/2019/07/15/us/joe-biden-busing-timeline.html

Chapter 2

1. *DeFunis v. Odegaard*, 416 U.S. 312, 331 (1974).
2. Ibid.
3. Adam Liptak, "The Memo That Rehnquist Wrote and Had to Disown," *New York Times*, September 11, 2005, https://www.nytimes.com/2005/09/11/weekinreview/the-memo-that-rehnquist-wrote-and-had-to-disown.html.
4. Anders Walker, "A Lawyer Looks at Civil Disobedience: How Lewis F. Powell, Jr. Reframed the Civil Rights Revolution," *University of Colorado Law Review* (2014), 5. https://scholarship.law.slu.edu/cgi/viewcontent.cgi?article=1168&context=faculty
5. Louis F. Powell Jr., "Civil Disobedience: Prelude to Revolution?," 40 *N.Y. St. B. J.* 40 (1968): 172, 181.
6. Lewis F. Powell Jr., "Soviet Education: Means Towards World Domination" (Report on Trip to Soviet Union, July–August 1958), Folder: A Means Toward World Domination, Box 27: Speeches & Writings, 1930–1962, Lewis F. Powell Jr. Archives, Washington & Lee University School of Law, Lexington, Virginia. Quoted in Walker, "A Lawyer Looks at Civil Disobedience," at 1238.
7. *Regents of the University of California v. Bakke*, 438 U.S. at 294 n. 34 (1978).
8. *Bakke*, 438 U.S. at 317–318.
9. *Bakke*, 438 U.S. at 326.
10. *Bakke*, 438 U.S. at 327.
11. *Bakke*, 438 U.S. at 387.
12. *Bakke*, 438 U.S. at 394.
13. *Bakke*, 438 U.S. at 400.
14. *Bakke*, 438 U.S. at 397.
15. Mary Wood, "Grutter Litigators Explain Strategies Used to Win Affirmative Action," University of Virginia School of Law, April 1, 2004, https://www.law.virginia.edu/news/2004_spr/grutter.htm.

16. Phillip Mericle, "Reagan Echoes Nixon's Anti-Busing Position," Richard Nixon Foundation, May 27, 2015, https://www.nixonfoundation.org/2015/05/rea gan-echoes-nixons-anti-busing-position.

17. "Reagan Quotes King Speech in Opposing Minority Quotas," *New York Times*, January 19, 1986, https://www.nytimes.com/1986/01/19/us/reagan-quo tes-king-speech-in-opposing-minority-quotas.html.

18. Justin Gomer and Christopher Petrella, "How the Reagan Administration Stoked Fears of Anti-White Racism," *Washington Post*, October 10, 2017, https://www.washingtonpost.com/news/made-by-history/wp/2017/10/ 10/how-the-reagan-administration-stoked-fears-of-anti-white-racism.

19. Francis X. Clines, "Watt Asks That Reagan Forgive 'Offensive' Remark About Panel," *New York Times*, September 23, 1983, https://www.nytimes.com/ 1983/09/23/us/watt-asks-that-reagan-forgive-offensive-remark-about-panel.html.

20. David Hoffman, "Watt Submits Resignation as Interior Secretary," *Washington Post*, October 10, 1983, https://www.washingtonpost.com/archive/politics/ 1983/10/10/watt-submits-resignation-as-interior-secretary/84ba758c-03f2-439d-8105-0bab802247b9.

21. Frank James, "Political Pro with Race-Baiting Past Doesn't See It in Romney's Welfare Charge," *NPR*, September 10, 2012, https://www.npr.org/sections/ itsallpolitics/2012/09/10/160885683/political-pro-with-race-baiting-past-doesnt-see-it-in-romneys-welfare-charge.

22. Peter Applebome, "The 1990 Elections: North Carolina; Helms Kindled Anger in Campaign, And May Have Set Tone for Others," *New York Times*, November 8, 1990, https://www.nytimes.com/1990/11/08/us/1990-electi ons-north-carolina-helms-kindled-anger-campaign-may-have-set-tone-for.html.

23. Thomas I. Palley, "The Forces Making for an Economic Collapse," *Atlantic*, July 1996, https://www.theatlantic.com/magazine/archive/1996/07/the-for ces-making-for-an-economic-collapse/376621/.

24. "The Productivity-Pay Gap," *Economic Policy Institute*, updated August 2021,https://www.epi.org/productivity-pay-gap/.

25. Ibid.

26. Ibid.

27. Kimberlé Crenshaw, "Race, Reform, and Retrenchment: Transformation and Legitimation in Antidiscrimination Law," *Harvard Law Review* 101, no. 7 (May 1988): 1361–1362, https://doi.org/10.2307/1341398.

28. *Ballotpedia*, s.v. "California Proposition 209, Affirmative Action Initiative (1996)," https://ballotpedia.org/California_Proposition_209,_Affirmative_ Action_Initiative_(1996).

29. *Ballotpedia*, s.v. "Article I, California Constitution: Section 31," https://ball otpedia.org/Article_I,_California_Constitution#Section_31.

30. University of California Board of Regents, "Regents Policy 4401: Policy on Future Admissions, Employment, and Contracting (Resolution Rescinding SP-1 and SP-2)," May, 16, 2001, https://perma.cc/9JNC-RP5B.

31. Thomas Peel and Daniel J. Willis, "Dropping Affirmative Action Had Huge Impact on California's Public Universities," *EdSource*, October 29, 2020, https://edsource.org/2020/dropping-affirmative-action-had-huge-impact-on-californias-public-universities/642437.

32. Melissa Korn and Christine Mai-Duc, "California Campaign to Revive Affirmative Action Is Struggling," *Wall Street Journal*, October 22, 2020, https://www.wsj.com/articles/california-campaign-to-revive-affirmative-act ion-is-struggling-11603364415.

33. Zachary Bleemer, "Affirmative Action, Mismatch, and Economic Mobility After California's Proposition 209," UC Berkeley Center for Studies in Higher Education, August 2020, https://cshe.berkeley.edu/sites/default/files/publi cations/rops.cshe.10.2020.bleemer.prop209.8.20.2020_2.pdf.

34. Stacy Berg Dale and Alan B. Krueger, "Estimating the Payoff to Attending a More Selective College: An Application of Selection on Observables and Unobservables," *Quarterly Journal of Economics* 117, no. 4 (November 2002): 1491–1527, https://doi.org/10.1162/003355302320935089.

35. Stacy Berg Dale and Alan B. Krueger, "Estimating the Return to College Selectivity over the Career Using Administrative Earnings Data" (working paper no. 17159, National Bureau of Economic Research, June 2011), doi. org/10.3386/w17159.

36. *Hopwood v. Texas*, No. A 92 CA 563 SS (W.D. Tex. July 24, 2001), https://tarl tonapps.law.utexas.edu/rare/documents/hopwood_district_courts_decis ion.pdf.

37. *Hopwood v. Texas*, 78 F.3d 932, 962 (5th Cir. 1996).

38. Ibid.

39. *Texas v. Hopwood*, 116 S. Ct. 2581, 2581–2582 (1996) (Ginsberg, J., concurring (respecting denial of petition for certiorari)).

40. "Gratz v. Bollinger; Grutter v. Bollinger," Center for Individual Rights, accessed May 20, 2022, https://www.cir-usa.org/cases/gratz-v-bollinger-grutter-v-bollinger.

41. Wendy Parker, "The Story of Grutter v. Bollinger: Affirmative Action Wins" (working paper no. 929706, Wake Forest University Legal Studies, May 4, 2009), doi.org/10.2139/ssrn.929706.

42. *Grutter v. Bollinger*, 137 F. Supp.2d 821 (E.D. Mich. 2001).

43. Gail Heriot, "Thoughts on Grutter v. Bollinger and Gratz v. Bollinger as Law and as Practical Politics," *Loyola University Chicago Law Journal* 35, no. 1 (Fall 2004): 140–141, https://lawecommons.luc.edu/cgi/viewcontent.cgi?arti cle=1246&context=luclj.

44. Wood, "Grutter Litigators."

45. Ibid.

46. Transcript of Oral Argument, *Grutter v. Bollinger*, No. 02-241, April 1, 2003, https://www.supremecourt.gov/oral_arguments/argument_transcripts/2002/02-241.pdf, 30–31.

47. Ibid., 31.

48. *Gratz v. Bollinger*, 539 U.S. 244, 271–272 (2003).

49. *Grutter v. Bollinger*, 539 U.S. 306, 319 (2003).

50. *Grutter*, 539 U.S. at 332.

51. Adam Winkler, "Fatal in Theory and Strict in Fact: An Empirical Analysis of Strict Scrutiny in the Federal Courts," *Vanderbilt Law Review* 59, no. 3 (April 2006): 793, https://scholarship.law.vanderbilt.edu/vlr/vol59/iss3/3.

52. *Grutter*, 539 U.S. at 344.

53. *Grutter*, 539 U.S. at 343.

54. Gordon Lloyd and Jenny S. Martinez, "The Slave Trade Clause," National Constitution Center, accessed May 20, 2022, https://constitutioncenter.org/interactive-constitution/interpretation/article-i/clauses/761.

55. *Grutter*, 539 U.S. at 345 (Ginsburg, J., concurring).

56. *Grutter*, 539 U.S. at 346 (Ginsburg, J., concurring).

57. *Grutter*, 539 U.S. at 349–350 (Thomas, J., concurring in part and dissenting in part), citing Fredrick Douglass, "What the Black Man Wants," transcript of a speech delivered at the Annual Meeting of the Massachusetts Anti-Slavery Society in Boston, January 26, 1865, https://www.blackpast.org/african-american-history/1865-frederick-douglass-what-black-man-wants (emphasis in original).

58. *Grutter*, 539 U.S. at 350.

59. *Grutter*, 539 U.S. at 353 (Thomas, J., concurring in part and dissenting in part).

60. *Grutter*, 539 U.S. at 367 (Thomas, J., concurring in part and dissenting in part).

61. *Grutter*, 539 U.S. at 383 (Rehnquist, C.J., dissenting).

62. David H. Gans, "Roberts at 10: Turning Back the Clock on Protections for Racial Equality," Constitutional Accountability Center, February 26, 2015, https://www.theusconstitution.org/wp-content/uploads/2017/12/Roberts_at_10_05_Racial_Equality_0.pdf.

63. "Oaths Taken by the Current Court," United States Supreme Court, accessed May 20, 2022, https://www.supremecourt.gov/about/oath/oathsofthecurrentcourt.aspx.

64. *Parents Involved in Cmty. Schs. v. Seattle Sch. Distr. No. 1*, 551 U.S. 701, 725 (2007).

65. *Parents Involved in Cmty. Schs.*, 551 U.S. at 788–789 (Kennedy, J., concurring).

66. *Parents Involved in Cmty. Schs.*, 551 U.S. at 724–725.

67. *Parents Involved in Cmty. Schs.*, 551 U.S. at 725.

68. *Parents Involved in Cmty. Schs.*, 551 U.S. at 721–722.

69. *Parents Involved in Cmty. Schs.*, 551 U.S. at 747–748.

70. Reva B. Siegel, "From Colorblindness to Antibalkanization: An Emerging Ground of Decision in Race Equality Cases," *Yale Law Journal* 120, no. 6 (April 2011): 1305, https://www.jstor.org/stable/41149567.

71. Linda Greenhouse, "Justices Limit the Use of Race in School Plans for Integration," *New York Times*, June 29, 2007, https://www.nytimes.com/2007/06/29/washington/29scotus.html.

72. *Parents Involved in Cmty. Schs.*, 551 U.S. at 803 (Stevens, J., dissenting).

73. *Fisher v. Univ. of Tex.*, 570 U.S. 297 (2013).

74. Mollie Reilly, "5 Things to Know About the Woman Whose Case Could End Affirmative Action as We Know It," *Huffington Post*, December 16, 2015, https://www.huffpost.com/entry/abigail-fisher-5-things-to-know_n_56719 717e4b0dfd4bcc026a4.

75. *Fisher*, 570 U.S. at 300.

76. Adam Liptak, "College Diversity Nears Its Last Stand," *New York Times*, October 15, 2011, https://www.nytimes.com/2011/10/16/sunday-review/college-diversity-nears-its-last-stand.html.

77. *Fisher*, 570 U.S. at 309.

78. *Fisher*, 570 U.S. at 309.

79. *Fisher*, 570 U.S. at 311.

80. *Fisher*, 570 U.S. at 308.

81. *Fisher v. Univ. of Tex.*, 579 U.S. 365, 377, 386 (2016).

82. *Fisher*, 579 U.S. at 388.

83. N'dea Yancey-Bragg, "'Righting Wrongs': Congress Is Taking Another Look at Reparations for Slavery," *USA Today*, February 17, 2021, https://www.usatoday.com/story/news/politics/2021/02/17/slavery-reparations-house-committee-debates-commission-study/6768395002.

84. Erica L. Green, Matt Apuzzo, and Katie Benner, "Trump Officials Reverse Obama's Policy on Affirmative Action in Schools," *New York Times*, July 3, 2018, https://www.nytimes.com/2018/07/03/us/politics/trump-affirmat ive-action-race-schools.html.

85. Borgna Brunner and Beth Rowen, "Timeline of Affirmative Action Milestones," Infoplease, updated January 25, 2021, https://www.infoplease.com/history/us/timeline-of-affirmative-action-milestones.

86. U.S. Const. amend. XIV, § 1.

87. Brief of Constitutional Law Scholars et al. as Amici Curiae in Support of Respondents, Fisher v. Univ. of Tex. at Austin, No. 14-981 (November 2, 2015).

88. Jack M. Balkin, *Living Originalism* (Cambridge, MA: Belknap Press of Harvard University Press); Siegel, "Federal Government's Power"; Eric Schnapper, "Affirmative Action and the Legislative History of the Fourteenth Amendment," *Virginia Law Review* 71, no. 5 (June 1985).

89. Siegel, "Federal Government's Power," 559.

90. Freedmen's Bureau Act, § 2, 14 Stat. 173, 174 (1866).
91. Act of March 3, 1865, § 5, 13 Stat. 510, 511.
92. Act of July 28, 1866, ch. 296, 14 Stat. 310, 317, a corporation created three years earlier by Congress.
93. Act of February 14, 1863, ch. 33, 12 Stat. 650, 650; as well as "for the relief of freedmen or destitute colored people in the District of Columbia," Resolution of March 16, 1867, No. 4, 15 Stat. 20.
94. See *Congressional Globe*, 39th Cong. 1st sess., December 5, 1865, p. 10, https://memory.loc.gov/cgi-bin/ampage (proposing that "[a]ll national and state laws shall be equally applicable to every citizen, and no discrimination shall be made on account of race and color"); Benjamin B. Kendrick, *The Journal of the Joint Committee of Fifteen on Reconstruction* (New York: Columbia University, 1914), 46 (proposing that "all laws, state or national, shall operate equally and impartially on all persons without regard to race or color") and 83 (proposing that "[n]o discrimination shall be made . . . as to the civil rights of persons because of race, color, or previous condition of servitude").

Chapter 3

1. Janelle Jones, John Schmitt, and Valerie Wilson, "50 Years After the Kerner Commission," Economic Policy Institute, February 26, 2018) https://files.epi.org/pdf/142084.pdf.
2. Ibid.
3. Ibid.
4. Richard Rothstein, "A 'Forgotten History' of How the U.S. Government Segregated America," interview by Terry Gross, *Fresh Air*, May 3, 2017, https://www.npr.org/2017/05/03/526655831/a-forgotten-history-of-how-the-u-s-government-segregated-america.
5. Tracy Hadden Loh, Christopher Coes, and Becca Buthe, "The Great Real Estate Reset; Separate and Unequal: Persistent Residential Segregation Is Sustaining Racial and Economic Injustice in the U.S," Brookings, December 16, 2020, https://www.brookings.edu/essay/trend-1-separate-and-unequal-neighborhoods-are-sustaining-racial-and-economic-injustice-in-the-us.
6. See also Rothstein, " 'Forgotten History' "; Devon Marisa Zuegel, "How We Subsidize Suburbia," *American Conservative*, October 20, 2017, https://www.theamericanconservative.com/urbs/we-have-always-subsidized-suburbia.
7. Sarah Pruitt, "The Post World War II Boom: How America Got into Gear," History Channel, May 14, 2020, https://www.history.com/news/post-world-war-ii-boom-economy.
8. Jones, Schmitt, and Wilson, *50 Years After the Kerner Commission*.
9. Ibid.

10. Anne Fisher, "Why Companies Are Saying Farewell to the 'Burbs, and Hello to the Big City," *Fortune*, June 24, 2015, https://fortune.com/2015/06/24/companies-moving-to-cities.

11. Kevin M. Kruse, *White Flight: Atlanta and the Making of Modern Conservatism* (Princeton: Princeton University Press, 2005), 244, https://www.google.com/books/edition/White_Flight/1aQoXxnENigC.

12. The National Advisory Commission on Civil Disorders, *The Kerner Report* (Princeton: Princeton University Press, 2016), 246.

13. Ibid.

14. "Public Housing History," National Low Income Housing Coalition, October 17, 2019, https://nlihc.org/resource/public-housing-history.

15. Jane Dailey, *Building the American Republic*, vol. 2, *A Narrative History from 1877* (Chicago: University of Chicago Press, 2018).

16. Ibid.

17. National Advisory Commission on Civil Disorders, Report, 1967, https://www.ojp.gov/ncjrs/virtual-library/abstracts/national-advisory-commission-civil-disorders-report.

18. Ibid.

19. Ibid.

20. "Timeline of Events in Shooting of Michael Brown in Ferguson," *AP News*, August 8, 2019, https://apnews.com/article/shootings-police-us-news-st-louis-michael-brown-9aa32033692547699a3b61da8fd1fc62.

21. *Encyclopedia Britannica*, s.v. "St. Louis, Missouri," by the Editors of Encyclopedia Britannica, updated November 19, 2021, https://www.britannica.com/place/Saint-Louis-Missouri.

22. Campbell Gibson and Kay Jung, "Historical Census Statistics on Population Totals by Race, 1790 to 1990, and by Hispanic Origin, 1970 to 1990, for Large Cities and Other Urban Places in the United States" (working paper no. 76, U.S. Census Bureau Population Division, February 2005), https://mcdc.missouri.edu/population-estimates/historical/POP-twps0076.pdf.

23. Richard Rothstein, *The Making of Ferguson: Public Policies at the Root of Its Troubles* (Economic Policy Institute, October 15, 2014), https://files.epi.org/2014/making-of-ferguson-final.pdf.

24. Ibid.

25. John Tucker, "10 of the Most Affluent African American Suburbs in the Nation," *Black Enterprise*, November 21, 2017, https://www.blackenterprise.com/10-affluent-african-american-suburbs.

26. U.S. Census Bureau, "Population Estimates, July 1 2021, (V2021)—Beverly Hills City, California," https://www.census.gov/quickfacts/fact/table/beverlyhillscitycalifornia#.

27. U.S. Census Bureau, "Population Estimates, July 1 2021, (V2021)—Bethesda CDP, Maryland," https://www.census.gov/quickfacts/bethesdacdpmaryland.

28. Tucker, " Most Affluent African American Suburbs."

29. Ann Choi, Keith Herbert, Arthur Browne, and Olivia Winslow, "Long Island Divided," *Newsday*, November 17, 2019, https://projects.newsday.com/long-island/real-estate-agents-investigation.

30. Jerusalem Demsas, "60 Percent of Likely Voters Say They're in Favor of Public Housing. So Why Isn't There More of It?," *Vox*, January 26, 2021, https://www.vox.com/22248779/affordable-housing-public-housing-poll-homel essness-crisis-covid-19-nimby-yimby-zoning.

31. Jacqueline Rabe Thomas, "Separated by Design: How Some of America's Richest Towns Fight Affordable Housing," *ProPublica*, May 22, 2019, https://www.propublica.org/article/how-some-of-americas-richest-towns-fight-aff ordable-housing.

32. Jacqueline Rabe Thomas, "Why Affordable Housing Is Built in Areas with High Crime, Few Jobs and Struggling Schools," *CTMirror*, December 1, 2019, https://www.ctpost.com/local/article/Why-affordable-housing-is-built-in-areas-with-14874116.php.

33. Carol Morello and Ted Mellnik, "Seven of Nation's 10 Most Affluent Counties Are in Washington Region," *Washington Post*, September 20, 2012, https://www.washingtonpost.com/local/seven-of-nations-10-most-affluent-count ies-are-in-washington-region/2012/09/19/f580bf30-028b-11e2-8102-ebe e9c66e190_story.html.

34. Dan Reed, "Residents of a Rich Montgomery County Neighborhood Provide a Helpful List of Places Where Cheaper Homes Can Go," *Greater Greater Washington*, August 31, 2021, https://ggwash.org/view/82377/rich-neigh borhood-provides-helpful-list-of-places-where-cheaper-homes-can-go.

35. John Park and Kyle Shelton, "Housing Choice Voucher Mobility in Houston," Kinder Institute for Urban Research, October 2019, https://doi.org/ 10.25611/29E9-9613.

36. Stephanie Wykstra, "Vouchers Can help the Poor Find Homes. But Landlords Often Won't Accept Them," *Vox*, December 10, 2019, https://www.vox.com/ future-perfect/2019/12/10/21001692/housing-vouchers-discrimination-racism-landlords.

37. Alison Bell, Barbara Sard, and Becky Koepnick, "Prohibiting Discrimination Against Renters Using Housing Vouchers Improves Results," Center on Budget and Priority Issues, December 20, 2018, https://www.cbpp.org/sites/ default/files/atoms/files/10-10-18hous.pdf.

38. Mary K. Cunningham "A Pilot Study of Landlord Acceptance of Housing Choice Vouchers," Urban Institute, August 20, 2018, https://www.urban. org/research/publication/pilot-study-landlord-acceptance-housing-choice-vouchers.

39. Connor Maxwell and Danyelle Solomon, "The Economic Fallout of the Coronavirus for People of Color," Center for American Progress, April 14,

2020, https://www.americanprogress.org/issues/race/news/2020/04/14/483125/economic-fallout-coronavirus-people-color.

40. Jamila Taylor, "Racism, Inequality, and Health Care for African Americans," The Century Foundation, December 19, 2019, https://tcf.org/content/report/racism-inequality-health-care-african-americans.

41. Alvin Chang, "The Data Proves That School Segregation Is Getting Worse," *Vox*, March 5, 2018,

42. Lee Bollinger, "Sixty Years Later, We Need a New Brown," *The New Yorker*, May 16, 2014, https://www.newyorker.com/news/news-desk/sixty-years-later-we-need-a-new-brown.

43. Laura Meckler, "Looking for His Ticket Out," *Washington Post*, updated October 12, 2020, https://www.washingtonpost.com/graphics/2020/national/george-floyd-america/education.

44. Chang, "Data Proves That School Segregation Is Getting Worse."

45. *San Antonio Indep. Sch. Dist. v. Rodriguez*, 411 U.S. 1 (1973).

46. Ibid.

47. Andrea Sachs, "The Worst Supreme Court Decisions Since 1960," *Time*, October 6, 2015, https://time.com/4056051/worst-supreme-court-decisions; David G. Savage, "How Did They Get It So Wrong?," *ABA Journal*, January 1, 2009, https://www.abajournal.com/magazine/article/how_did_they_get_it_so_wrong.

48. Nikole Hannah-Jones, "The Resegregation of Jefferson County," *New York Times*, September 6, 2017, https://www.nytimes.com/2017/09/06/magazine/the-resegregation-of-jefferson-county.html.

49. United Negro College Fund, "K-12 Disparity Facts and Statistics," accessed May 25, 2022, https://uncf.org/pages/k-12-disparity-facts-and-stats.

50. Clare Lombardo, "Why White School Districts Have So Much More Money," *NPR*, February 26, 2019, https://www.npr.org/2019/02/26/696794821/why-white-school-districts-have-so-much-more-money; see also Anna North, "How School Funding Can Help Repair the Legacy of Segregation," *Vox*, February 17, 2021, https://www.vox.com/22266219/biden-eduation-school-funding-segregation-antiracist-policy.

51. United Negro College Fund, "K-12 Disparity Facts and Statistics."

52. Chang, "Data Proves That School Segregation Is Getting Worse."

53. Janie Boschma and Ronald Brownstein, "The Concentration of Poverty in American Schools," *Atlantic*, February 26, 2016, https://www.theatlantic.com/education/archive/2016/02/concentration-poverty-american-schools/471414.

54. "Fast Facts: SAT Scores," National Center for Education Statistics, https://nces.ed.gov/fastfacts/display.asp?id=171.

55. "Fast Facts: Dropout Rates," National Center for Education Statistics, https://nces.ed.gov/fastfacts/display.asp?id=16.

56. United Negro College Fund, "K-12 Disparity Facts and Statistics."

57. Jennifer Cheeseman Day, "88% of Blacks Have a High School Diploma, 26% a Bachelor's Degree," United States Census Bureau, June 10, 2020, https://www.census.gov/library/stories/2020/06/black-high-school-attainment-nearly-on-par-with-national-average.html.

58. Jones, Schmitt, and Wilson, "50 Years After the Kerner Commission."

59. Ashkenas, Park, and Pearce, "Even with Affirmative Action," *New York Times*, August 24, 2017, https://www.nytimes.com/interactive/2017/08/24/us/affirmative-action.html.

60. Mark Huelsman, "Social Exclusion: The State of State U for Black Students," Demos, December 2018, 6, https://www.demos.org/sites/default/files/publications/SocialExclusion_StateOf.pdf.

61. Lauren Lumpkin, Meredith Kolodner, and Nick Anderson, "Flagship Universities Say Diversity Is a Priority. But Black Enrollment in Many States Continues to Lag," *Washington Post*, April 18, 2021, https://www.washingtonpost.com/education/2021/04/18/flagship-universities-black-enrollment.

62. Huelsman, "Social Exclusion," 6.

63. Judith Scott-Clayton and Jing Li, "Black-White Disparity in Student Loan Debt More Than Triples After Graduation," Brookings, October 20, 2016, https://www.brookings.edu/research/black-white-disparity-in-student-loan-debt-more-than-triples-after-graduation.

64. Taylor, "Racism, Inequality, and Health Care."

65. Ibid.

66. Andre M. Perry, Joia Crear-Perry, Carl Romer, and Nana Adjeiwaa-Manu, "The Racial Implications of Medical Debt: How Moving Toward Universal Health Care and Other Reforms Can Address Them," Brookings, October 5, 2021, https://www.brookings.edu/research/the-racial-implications-of-medical-debt-how-moving-toward-universal-health-care-and-other-reforms-can-address-them.

67. Federal Centers for Disease Control and Prevention, "Adult Obesity Facts," updated May 17, 2022, https://www.cdc.gov/obesity/data/adult.html.

68. Federal Centers for Disease Control and Prevention, "Facts About Hypertension," updated September 27, 2021, https://www.cdc.gov/bloodpressure/facts.htm.

69. Federal Centers for Disease Control and Prevention, "Infant Mortality," updated September 8, 2021, https://www.cdc.gov/reproductivehealth/maternalinfanthealth/infantmortality.htm.

70. Federal Centers for Disease Control and Prevention, "Coronary Heart Disease, Myocardial Infarction, and Stroke—A Public Health Issue," updated July 30, 2019, https://www.cdc.gov/aging/publications/coronary-heart-disease-brief.html.

71. Federal Centers for Disease Control and Prevention, "Most Recent National Asthma Data," updated March 30, 2021, https://www.cdc.gov/asthma/most_recent_national_asthma_data.htm.
72. U.S. Department of Health and Human Services Office of Minority Health, "Cancer and African Americans," updated August 26, 2021, https://minorityhealth.hhs.gov/omh/browse.aspx?lvl=4&lvlid=16.
73. Dora Hughes, "Why Are More Black Americans Dying of COVID-19?," interview by Shanoor Seervai, *The Dose*, Commonwealth Fund, June 26, 2020, https://www.commonwealthfund.org/publications/podcast/2020/jun/why-are-more-black-americans-dying-covid-19.
74. Julie Bosman, Sophie Kasakove, and Daniel Victor, "U.S. Life Expectancy Plunged in 2020, Especially for Black and Hispanic Americans," *New York Times*, July 21, 2021, https://www.nytimes.com/2021/07/21/us/american-life-expectancy-report.html.
75. Taylor, "Racism, Inequality, and Health Care."
76. Nada Hassenein, "Young Black Men and Teens Are Killed by Guns 20 Times More Than Their White Counterparts, CDC Data Shows," *USA Today*, February 23, 2021, https://www.usatoday.com/story/news/health/2021/02/23/young-black-men-teens-made-up-more-than-third-2019-gun-homicides/4559929001.
77. Juliana Menasce Horowitz, Anna Brown, and Rachel Minkin, "A Year into the Pandemic, Long-Term Financial Impact Weighs Heavily on Many Americans," Pew Research Center, March 5, 2021, https://www.pewresearch.org/social-trends/2021/03/05/a-year-into-the-pandemic-long-term-financial-impact-weighs-heavily-on-many-americans.
78. Aria Florent, J. P. Julien, Shelley Stewart, Nina Yancy, and Jason Wright, The Case for Accelerating Financial Inclusion in Black Communities, McKinsey and Company, February 25, 2020, https://www.mckinsey.com/industries/public-and-social-sector/our-insights/the-case-for-accelerating-financial-inclusion-in-black-communities.
79. Florent et al., "Case for Accelerating Financial Inclusion."
80. Lisa Rice and Erich Schwartz Jr., "Discrimination When Buying a Car: How the Color of Your Skin Can Affect Your Car-Shopping Experience," National Fair Housing Alliance, January 2018, https://nationalfairhousing.org/wp-content/uploads/2018/01/Discrimination-When-Buying-a-Car-FINAL-1-11-2018.pdf.
81. Signe-Mary McKernan, Caroline Ratcliffe, and C. Eugene Steuerle, "Wealth Inequalities," Urban Institute, September 2015, https://www.urban.org/policy-centers/cross-center-initiatives/inequality-and-mobility/projects/wealth-inequalities.
82. Florent et al., "Case for Accelerating Financial Inclusion."
83. Jones, Schmitt, and Wilson, "50 Years After the Kerner Commission."

84. Florent et al., "Case for Accelerating Financial Inclusion."
85. Christian E. Weller and Richard Figueroa, "Wealth Matters: The Black-White Wealth Gap Before and During the Pandemic," Center for American Progress, July 28, 2021, https://www.americanprogress.org/article/wealth-matters-black-white-wealth-gap-pandemic.
86. U.S. Bureau of Labor Statistics, "Unemployment Rate 3.6 Percent in April 2019, Lowest Since December 1969," May 8, 2019, https://www.bls.gov/opub/ted/2019/unemployment-rate-3-point-6-percent-in-april-2019-lowest-since-december-1969.htm.
87. U.S. Bureau of Labor Statistics, "Labor Force Characteristics by Race and Ethnicity, 2019," December 2020, https://www.bls.gov/opub/reports/race-and-ethnicity/2019/pdf/home.pdf.
88. U.S. Census Bureau, "Population Estimates, July 1 2021, (V2021)—United States," https://www.census.gov/quickfacts/fact/table/US/PST045219.
89. Olugbenga Ajilore, "The Persistent Black-White Unemployment Gap Is Built into the Labor Market," Center for American Progress, September 28, 2020, https://www.americanprogress.org/issues/economy/news/2020/09/28/490702/persistent-black-white-unemployment-gap-built-labor-market.
90. Patrick Bayer and Kerwin Kofi Charles, "Divergent Paths: Structural Change, Economic Rank, and the Evolution of Black-White Earnings Differences, 1940–2014" (working paper no. 222797, National Bureau of Economic Research, revised September 2017), https://www.nber.org/system/files/working_papers/w22797/w22797.pdf.
91. Taylor Nicole Rogers, "There Are 614 Billionaires in the United States, and Only 7 of Them Are Black," Insider, updated September 4, 2020, https://www.businessinsider.com/black-billionaires-in-the-united-states-2020-2.
92. "Robert F. Smith," Forbes, updated May 26, 2022, https://www.forbes.com/profile/robert-f-smith/?sh=3451859c2236.
93. Florent et al., "The Case for Accelerating Financial Inclusion."
94. Dailey, Building the American Republic, 266.
95. Lincoln Quillian, Devah Pager, Arnfinn H. Midtbøen, and Ole Hexel, "Hiring Discrimination Against Black Americans Hasn't Declined in 25 Years," Harvard Business Review, October 11, 2017, https://hbr.org/2017/10/hiring-discrimination-against-black-americans-hasnt-declined-in-25-years.
96. U.S. Bureau of Labor Statistics, "Labor Force Statistics from the Current Population Survey," January 2020, https://www.bls.gov/cps/cpsaat11.htm .
97. Jeanne Sahadi, "After Years of Talking About Diversity, the Number of Black Leaders at US Companies Is Still Dismal," CNN, updated June 2, 2020, https://www.cnn.com/2020/06/02/success/diversity-and-black-leadership-in-corporate-america/index.html.
98. Ibid.
99. Ibid.

100. Jessica DiNapoli, "Black Americans, Women Make Big Strides on Top U.S. Corporate Boards," *Reuters*, October 19, 2021, https://www.reuters.com/world/us/black-americans-women-make-big-strides-top-us-corporate-boards-report-2021-10-19.
101. Ibid.
102. *Reynolds v. Sims*, 377 U.S. 533, 562 (1964).
103. Carnegie Corporation, "Voting Rights: A Short History," Carnegie Corporation of New York, November 18, 2019, https://www.carnegie.org/our-work/article/voting-rights-timeline/.
104. *Shelby Cnty., Ala. v. Holder*, 570 U.S. 529, 571 (2013) (Ginsburg, J., dissenting) (citing H.R. Rep. No. 109–478, at 21 (2006)).
105. *Shelby Cnty.*, 570 U.S. at 536, 547.
106. *Shelby Cnty.*, 570 U.S. at 590 (Ginsburg, J., dissenting).
107. Greg Abbott (@GregAbbott_TX), "Texas #VoterID law should go into effect immediately b/c #SCOTUS struck down section 4 of VRA today. #txlege #tcot #txgop," Twitter, June 25, 2013, 9:19 A.M., https://twitter.com/GregAbbott_TX/status/349532390336643075.
108. *Ballotpedia*, s.v. "North Carolina Voter ID Amendment (2018)," https://ballotpedia.org/North_Carolina_Voter_ID_Amendment_(2018).
109. U.S. Commission on Civil Rights, *An Assessment of Minority Voting Rights Access in the United States: 2018 Statutory Enforcement Report*, September 2018, https://www.usccr.gov/files/pubs/2018/Minority_Voting_Access_2018.pdf.
110. *Brnovich v. Democratic Nat'l Comm.*, 141 S. Ct. 2321 (2021).
111. *Brnovich*, 141 S. Ct. at 2362 (Kagan, J., dissenting).
112. *Brnovich*, 141 S. Ct. at 2362 (emphasis added).
113. "Brnovich v. Democratic National Committee," *Harvard Law Review* 135, no. 1 (November 2021), https://harvardlawreview.org/2021/11/brnovich-v-democratic-national-committee.
114. Geoffrey Skelley, "How the Republican Push to Restrict Voting Could Affect Our Elections," *FiveThirtyEight*, May 17, 2021, https://fivethirtyeight.com/features/how-the-republican-push-to-restrict-voting-could-affect-our-elections.
115. "Police Shootings Database, 2015–2022," *Washington Post*, updated May 24, 2022, https://www.washingtonpost.com/graphics/investigations/police-shootings-database.
116. Radley Balko, "There's Overwhelming Evidence That the Criminal Justice System Is Racist. Here's the Proof," *Washington Post*, June 10, 2020, https://www.washingtonpost.com/graphics/2020/opinions/systemic-racism-police-evidence-criminal-justice-system.
117. Susan Nembhard and Lily Robin, *Racial and Ethnic Disparities Throughout the Criminal Legal System: A Result of Racist Policies and Discretionary Practices*,

Urban Institute, August 2021, https://www.urban.org/sites/default/files/publication/104687/racial-and-ethnic-disparities-throughout-the-criminal-legal-system.pdf.

118. Balko, "Overwhelming Evidence."

119. Paul Duggan, "A Disproportionate Number of D.C. Police Stops Involved African Americans," *Washington Post*, September 9, 2019, https://www.washingtonpost.com/local/public-safety/a-disproportionate-number-of-dc-police-stops-involved-african-americans/2019/09/09/6f11beb0-d347-11e9-9343-40db57cf6abd_story.html.

120. Balko, "Overwhelming Evidence."

121. Ibid.

122. American Civil Liberties Union, "Mass Incarceration," https://www.aclu.org/issues/smart-justice/mass-incarceration.

123. Balko, "Overwhelming Evidence."

124. United States Sentencing Commission, "Demographic Differences in Sentencing," November 4, 2017, https://www.ussc.gov/research/research-reports/demographic-differences-sentencing.

125. Balko, "Overwhelming Evidence."

126. Jeremy Travis, Bruce Western, and Steve Redburn, eds., *The Growth of Incarceration in the United States: Exploring Causes and Consequences* (Washington, DC: National Academies Press, 2014), 33, https://www.nap.edu/read/18613/chapter/4.

127. Ashley Nellis, *The Color of Justice: Racial and Ethnic Disparity in State Prisons*, The Sentencing Project, October 2021, https://www.sentencingproject.org/wp-content/uploads/2016/06/The-Color-of-Justice-Racial-and-Ethnic-Disparity-in-State-Prisons.pdf.

128. Todd D. Minton and Zhen Zeng, *Jail Inmates in 2020: Statistical Tables*, NCJ 303308, Bureau of Justice Statistics, December 2021, https://bjs.ojp.gov/content/pub/pdf/ji20st.pdf.

129. "President Nixon Declares Drug Abuse 'Public Enemy Number One,'" Richard Nixon Society, recording of July 17, 1971, press conference in Washington, DC, uploaded April 29, 2016, https://www.youtube.com/watch?v=y8TGLLQlD9M.

130. Dan Baum, "Legalize It All," *Harper's*, April 2016, https://harpers.org/archive/2016/04/legalize-it-all.

131. U.S. Department of Justice, "Comprehensive Crime Control Act of 1984," https://www.ojp.gov/ncjrs/virtual-library/abstracts/comprehensive-crime-control-act-1984-0.

132. Elizabeth Hinton, *From the War on Crime to the War on Drugs* (Cambridge, MA: Harvard University Press, 2017), 309.

133. Hinton, *From the War on Crime*, 307–334.

134. Roy Walmsley, *World Prison Population List*, 12th ed. (London: Institute for Criminal Policy Research, 2018), https://www.prisonstudies.org/sites/defa ult/files/resources/downloads/wppl_12.pdf.

135. Federal Bureau of Prisons, "Inmate Race," updated May 21, 2022, https:// www.bop.gov/about/statistics/statistics_inmate_race.jsp.

136. Elizabeth Hinton, LeShae Henderson, and Cindy Reed, *An Unjust Burden: The Disparate Treatment of Black Americans in the Criminal Justice System* (New York: Vera Institute of Justice, May 2018), https://www.vera.org/downlo ads/publications/for-the-record-unjust-burden-racial-disparities.pdf.

137. Juleyka Lantigua-Williams, "The Link Between Race and Solitary Confinement," *Atlantic*, December 5, 2016, https://www.theatlantic.com/ politics/archive/2016/12/race-solitary-confinement/509456.

138. Death Penalty Information Center, "DPIC Analysis: Racial Disparities Persisted in U.S. Death Sentences and Executions in 2019," January 21, 2020, https://deathpenaltyinfo.org/news/dpic-analysis-racial-disparities-persis ted-in-the-u-s-death-sentences-and-executions-in-2019.

139. Death Penalty Information Center, "Executions by Race and Race of Victim," accessed May 29, 2022, https://deathpenaltyinfo.org/executions/executi ons-overview/executions-by-race-and-race-of-victim.

140. John Gramlich, "The Gap Between the Number of Blacks and Whites in Prison Is Shrinking," Pew Research Center, April 30, 2019, https://www. pewresearch.org/fact-tank/2019/04/30/shrinking-gap-between-number-of-blacks-and-whites-in-prison.

Chapter 4

1. Campbell Gibson and Kay Jung, "Historical Census Statistics on Population Totals by Race, 1790 to 1990, and By Hispanic Origin, 1970 to 1990, for the United States, Regions, Divisions, and States," working paper no. 56, U.S. Census Bureau Population Division, September 2002, https://www.cen sus.gov/content/dam/Census/library/working-papers/2002/demo/POP-twps0056.pdf.

2. "Immigration and Nationality Act of 1965," United States House of Representatives: History, Art, and Archives, accessed May 29, 2022, https:// history.house.gov/Historical-Highlights/1951-2000/Immigration-and-Nati onality-Act-of-1965.

3. U.S. Census Bureau, "Quick Facts, United States" (V2021), https://www.cen sus.gov/quickfacts/fact/table/US/PST045221.

4. Dione J. Pierre, "Demands for Segregated Housing at Williams College Are Not News," *National Review*, May 8, 2019, https://www.nationalreview.com/ 2019/05/american-colleges-segregated-housing-graduation-ceremonies.

5. Deborah Son Holoien, "Do Differences Make a Difference? The Effects of Diversity on Learning, Intergroup Outcomes, and Civic Engagement," Princeton University Trsutee Ad Hoc Committee on Diversity Report, September 2013, https://inclusive.princeton.edu/sites/g/files/toruqf1831/files/pu-report-diversity-outcomes.pdf; Emily J. Shaw, "Researching the Educational Benefits of Diversity," College Board Research Report No. 2005-4, 2005, https://files.eric.ed.gov/fulltext/ED562839.pdf.

6. Claude M. Steele, "Thin Ice: Stereotype Threat and Black College Students," *Atlantic*, August 1999, https://www.theatlantic.com/magazine/archive/1999/08/thin-ice-stereotype-threat-and-black-college-students/304663.

7. Claude M. Steele, *Whistling Vivaldi: How Stereotypes Affect Us and What We Can Do* (New York: W. W. Norton, 2011), 135. Per Steele, social identity threat is defined as the concern people have in situations in which the positive image of their ingroup is threatened by the activation of negative group stereotypes, or by the devaluation or stigmatization of the ingroup. See also Claude M. Steele, Steven J. Spencer, and Joshua Aronson, "Contending with Group Image: The Psychology of Stereotype and Social Identity Threat," *Advances in Experimental Social Psychology* 34 (2002): 379–440, https://doi.org/10.1016/S0065-2601(02)80009-0.

8. Steele, *Whistling Vivaldi*, 137.

9. Matthew M. Chingos, "Are Minority Students Harmed by Affirmative Action?," Brookings, March 7, 2013, https://www.brookings.edu/research/are-minority-students-harmed-by-affirmative-action.

10. William G. Bowen, Matthew M. Chingos, and Michael S. McPherson, *Crossing the Finish Line: Completing College at America's Public Universities* (Princeton: Princeton University Press, 2009), 210.

11. Chingos, "Are Minority Students Harmed by Affirmative Action?"

12. Brief of the American Educational Research Association et al. as Amici Curiae in Support of Respondents, *Fisher v. Univ. of Tex. at Austin*, No. 11-345, August 13, 2012, https://www.scotusblog.com/wp-content/uploads/2016/08/11-345-respondent-amicus-AERA.pdf.

13. Mary J. Fischer, "Does Campus Diversity Promote Friendship Diversity? A Look at Interracial Friendships in College," *Social Science Quarterly* 89, no. 3 (September 2008): https://doi.org/10.1111/j.1540-6237.2008.00552.x.

14. Nicholas A. Bowman, "College Diversity Experiences and Cognitive Development: A Meta-Analysis," *Review of Educational Research* 80, no. 1 (March 2010): https://www.jstor.org/stable/40658444.

15. Uma Jayakumar, "Can Higher Education Meet the Needs of an Increasingly Diverse and Global Society? Campus Diversity and Cross-Cultural Workforce Competencies," *Harvard Educational Review* 78, no. 4 (2008): https://doi.org/10.17763/haer.78.4.b60031p350276699.

16. Nicholas A. Bowman, "Promoting Participation in a Diverse Democracy: A Meta-Analysis of College Diversity Experiences and Civic Engagement," *Review of Educational Research* 81, no. 1 (2011): https://doi.org/10.3102%2F0 034654310383047.

17. James Sidanius, Shana Levin, Colette van Laar, and David O. Sears, *The Diversity Challenge: Social Identity and Intergroup Relations on the College Campus* (New York: Russell Sage Foundation, 2008), https://www.google. com/books/edition/The_Diversity_Challenge/CPsWAwAAQBAJ; Brief of the American Educational Research Association et al. as Amici Curiae in Support of Respondents, *Fisher v. Univ. of Tex. at Austin*, No. 14-981, October 30, 2015, https://www.scotusblog.com/wp-content/uploads/2015/11/14-981bsacAmericanEducationalResearchAssociationEtAl.pdf.

18. Deirdre M. Bowen, "Brilliant Disguise: An Empirical Analysis of a Social Experiment Banning Affirmative Action," *Indiana Law Journal* 85, no. 4 (Fall 2010): https://www.repository.law.indiana.edu/cgi/viewcontent.cgi?article= 1034&context=ilj.

19. Ibid., at 1198.

20. Ibid.

21. John Creamer, "Inequalities Persist Despite Decline in Poverty for All Major Race and Hispanic Origin Groups," United States Census Bureau, September 15, 2020, https://www.census.gov/library/stories/2020/09/poverty-rates-for-blacks-and-hispanics-reached-historic-lows-in-2019.html.

22. Alan Krueger, Jesse Rothstein, and Sarah Turner, "Race, Income, and College in 25 Years: Evaluating Justice O'Connor's Conjecture," *American Law and Economics Review* 8, no. 2 (Summer 2006): https://doi.org/10.1093/aler/ ahl004.

23. Anthony P. Carnevale and Jeff Strohl, "Separate and Unequal: How Higher Education Reinforces the Intergenerational Reproduction of White Racial Privilege," Georgetown Public Policy Institute, July 2013, 37–38, https://cew. georgetown.edu/wp-content/uploads/SeparateUnequal.FR_.pdf.

24. Sigal Alon, *Race, Class, and Affirmative Action* (New York: Russell Sage Foundation, 2015), 176.

25. Brief of 823 Social Scientists as Amici Curiae in Support of Respondents, *Fisher v. Univ. of Tex. at Austin*, No. 14-981, October 30, 2015, https://www. scotusblog.com/wp-content/uploads/2015/11/14-981_amicus_resp_82 3Social-Scientists.authcheckdam.pdf; see also Sean F. Reardon, Rachel Baker, Matt Kasman, Daniel Klasik, and Joseph Townsend, "Can Socioeconomic Status Substitute for Race in Affirmative Action College Admissions Policies? Evidence from a Simulation Model," Educational Testing Service, 2015, 21– 22, https://www.ets.org/Media/Research/pdf/reardon_white_paper.pdf.

26. Ted Mellnik and Carol Morello, "Washington: A World Apart," *Washington Post*, November 9, 2013, https://www.washingtonpost.com/sf/local/2013/11/09/washington-a-world-apart.

27. Lynne DeAmelio-Rafferty, "How Much Do College Applications Cost?," Edmit, December 2, 2018, https://www.edmit.me/blog/how-much-do-college-applications-cost.

28. Andy Olin, "There Are Only 19 Prosperous Majority-Black ZIP Codes in the US. The Houston Area Is Home to Two," Kinder Institute for Urban Research, January 13, 2021, https://kinder.rice.edu/urbanedge/2021/01/13/19-prosperous-majority-black-zip-codes-us-two-in-houston-disparity.

29. Saul Geiser, "SAT/ACT Scores, High-School GPA, and the problem of Omitted Variable Bias: Why the UC Taskforce's Findings Are Spurious," Center for Studies in Higher Education, March 2020, https://vcresearch.berkeley.edu/research-unit/center-studies-higher-education#:~:text=The%20Center%20for%20Studies%20in,nation%2C%20and%20comparative%20international%20issues.

30. Lee Bollinger in conversation with Claude Steele.

31. Isabel Wilkerson, *Caste: The Origins of Our Discontent* (New York: Random House, 2020), 106.

32. Students for Fair Admissions, "About," accessed May 30, 2022, https://studentsforfairadmissions.org/about.

33. Lawyer's Committee for Civil Rights Under Law, "Students for Fair Admissions (SFFA) v. Harvard," accessed May 30, 2022, https://www.lawyerscommittee.org/students-for-fair-admissions-sffa-v-harvard.

34. Brief for the United States as Amicus Curiae, *Students for Fair Admissions, Inc. v. President and Fellows of Harvard College*, No. 20-1199, December 8, 2021, https://www.supremecourt.gov/DocketPDF/20/20-1199/204668/20211209161118061_20-1199%20-%20SFFA%20v%20Harvard%20CVSG%20-%20Corrected.pdf.

35. Meera E. Deo, "The End of Affirmative Action," *North Carolina Law Review* 100 (December 2021): https://papers.ssrn.com/sol3/papers.cfm?abstract_id=3810391.

36. Anemona Hartocollis, "The Affirmative Action Battle at Harvard Is Not Over," *New York Times*, February 18, 2020, https://www.nytimes.com/2020/02/18/us/affirmative-action-harvard.html.

37. Lawyers' Committee for Civil Rights Under Law, "Students for Fair Admissions (SFFA) v. Harvard."

38. Nick Anderson, "Justice Department Argues Harvard's Use of Race in Admissions Violates Civil Rights Law," *Washington Post*, February 26, 2020, https://www.washingtonpost.com/education/2020/02/26/justice-department-argues-harvards-use-race-admissions-violates-civil-rights-law.

39. Brief for the United States as Amicus Curiae, *Students for Fair Admissions, Inc. v. President and Fellows of Harvard College.*

40. Lawyer's Committee for Civil Rights Under Law, "Students for Fair Admissions (SFFA) v. University of North Carolina at Chapel Hill," accessed May 30, 2022, https://www.lawyerscommittee.org/students-for-fair-admissions-sffa-v-harvard.

41. Jamelle Bouie, "Easy AA," *Slate*, June 29, 2015, https://slate.com/news-and-politics/2015/06/fisher-v-university-of-texas-the-supreme-court-might-just-gut-affirmative-action-this-time.html.

42. Lorenzo Arvanitis and Serena Cho, "Kavanaugh Poses a Potential Threat for Affirmative Action, Experts Say," *Yale Daily News*, October 15, 2018, https://yaledailynews.com/blog/2018/10/15/kavanaugh-poses-a-potential-threat-for-affirmative-action-experts-say.

43. Eric Foner, author of *Reconstruction: America's Unfinished Journey*, in a talk to the Century Association, February 2018 (YouTube: https://www.youtube.com/watch?v=49McwjkZmlw).

44. *Schuette v. Coalition to Defend Affirmative Action*, 572 U.S. 291, 380–381 (2014) (Sotomayor, J., dissenting).

45. Jay Caspian King, "The Case Against 'Excellence' at Universities," *New York Times*, September 13, 2021, https://www.nytimes.com/2021/09/13/opinion/SAT-universities-admissions.html.

INDEX

For the benefit of digital users, indexed terms that span two pages (e.g., 52–53) may, on occasion, appear on only one of those pages.